On Approval

A comedy

Frederick Lonsdale

Samuel French — London

CHARACTERS

The Duke of Bristol
Richard Halton
Mrs Wislack
Helen Hayle

SYNOPSIS OF SCENES

ACT I
Helen's house in Mayfair, London. August

ACTS II and III
Mrs Wislack's house in Scotland. September

Three weeks elapse between Acts I and II
Three hours elapse between Acts II and III

ON APPROVAL

ACT I

SCENE.—HELEN'S *house in Mayfair, London.*

(HELEN *enters door* R. *She turns at the door and looks off stage; voices can be heard arguing. She smiles to herself and goes slowly across to the back of the table* L. *of* C., *and pours out coffee.* MRS. WISLACK (MARIA) *follows as* HELEN *reaches her position at the table.* MARIA *is obviously very angry.*)

MARIA (*slamming the door, then turning to* HELEN). I—I—hope his cigar chokes him!

HELEN (*pouring out coffee*). Darling, you take him too seriously.

MARIA. Do I? (*Moving across in front to up* L. *of* HELEN *at table.*) If he were not a duke, no one would know him! The beast!

HELEN (*hands her coffee*). But what did he do that's annoyed you so much?

MARIA. From the moment we sat down to dinner, his only conversation was women over forty.

HELEN. Then you could never have been in his mind, because he kept saying you were only thirty-eight!

MARIA. I was born on the same day as his stepmother, and that damn woman couldn't keep her mouth shut about anything! Oh, how I dislike him! (*Moves to settee* R.C. *and sits at its* R. *end.*)

HELEN. How ridiculous you are! Liqueur?

MARIA (*shaking her head*). Even as a boy he was unpleasant; if he hadn't been a duke and we hadn't been snobs, not one of us would have even dared to take him on our knee! Hideous child, how I detested him!

HELEN. I'm sorry, because I like him so much.

MARIA. That reminds me! Why is he always dining here?

HELEN. I have told you, I like him so much!

MARIA. You wouldn't marry him?

HELEN. How far is it from here in a taxi to St. George's, Hanover Square?

MARIA. Ten minutes. Why?

HELEN. If he asked me to marry him to-night, I'd undertake to run it in five.

5

MARIA. Helen, you're mad!

HELEN. Am I? It's an attractive complaint. (*She moves round the* L. *end of the table.*)

MARIA. But—but he literally hasn't a penny in the world!

HELEN. My father was a far-seeing man; he bottled some pickles. (*She sits in the chair* L. *of table.*)

MARIA. Give me some brandy!

(HELEN *half rises.*)

No, no, I don't want any!

(HELEN *sits again.*)

This is terrible, terrible! Will you believe me if I tell you that he hasn't one penny in the world, and if he married you it will only be for your money?

HELEN (*rises and moves to her*). I can't see that that makes him very terrible! A lot of women have lived with him for his!

MARIA. Keep silent a moment, I think I'm going to have a stroke! What do you see in the brute?

HELEN. Everything! He's not bad-looking, has a charming voice. He's witty, and I adore him! (*Takes coffee cup from* MARIA *and moves to the front of table.*)

MARIA. If you married him, in a year you would find he is none of those things.

HELEN (*turns*). I should?

MARIA. Nineteen years ago I was asked in a church if I would take a man to be my wedded husband, and I answered "yes." I looked at him and believed he looked and was everything that he wasn't; he then drove me home, for the purpose of proving to me that he was everything that he was!

HELEN (*in front of table. Laughs*). You needn't be the least bit alarmed. The reason the Duke of Bristol comes here so often is—he's fond of my cook, he approves of my champagne, my cigars are in perfect condition, and my coffee is the only coffee worth drinking—but to me personally, he is entirely indifferent—I don't exist!

MARIA. Thank God!

HELEN. That's cruel of you! (*Turning to her.*)

MARIA. The reverse, it's kind of me!—a girl of twenty-two, an orphan, and one of the richest women in England, you're at the mercy of any man like him!

HELEN (*sitting* L. *end of the settee*). Then even if you loved someone terribly, you would never marry again?

MARIA. I don't say that; but if I ever do, I shall require to know a great deal more about the next one than I did about the last! (*She rises and moves to* C.)

HELEN. I don't see how that can *ever* be done!

MARIA. It can! I should take him away alone for one month on approval.

HELEN (*laughing*). But, Maria, darling, supposing at the end of the month you found you didn't like him, what would you do then ?

MARIA. Give him his railway fare and send him home again! (*She moves to* L.)

HELEN. Wouldn't your position be a little embarrassing ?

MARIA. Not in the least! I should give him clearly to understand when we started that I was taking him away only to find out if he loved me for myself alone ; if when we were away I found I had not convinced him that was the case, I should then in a subtle way prove to him I was one of the few women in England who could use a revolver accurately.

HELEN (*smiling*). Would your women friends believe that ?

MARIA. Ninety-six per cent of my women friends hate revolvers !

HELEN (*rising and moving up stage*). I wish you would do it, darling. It would be a marvellous precedent for other women if you did ! (*She sits at the piano.*)

MARIA (*looking towards the door* R.). I am thinking very seriously of doing it !

HELEN. You don't mean that ?

MARIA (*moving up to the front of table*). At your table to-night there was a man——

HELEN (*who has just touched the keys—turns*). Richard !

MARIA (*sitting on the edge of the table*). Richard, whom I have known all my life, and who, ever since I have known him, has for causes of shyness or lack of means not been able to quite tell me that he loves me !

HELEN. I have always believed he adores you ! And he's one of the nicest men in the world !

MARIA. On the surface he appears everything that is desirable. But married to him, he may be none of those things ! That is what I am thinking seriously of finding out !

HELEN. You are going to take *him* away on approval ?

MARIA. I say I may ! Of course there—— (*Hearing the men approaching.*) Careful !

(*The* DUKE *and* RICHARD *enter from door* R. RICHARD *goes up* R. *The* DUKE *crosses to* C.)

DUKE. Well, here we are ! (*Coming to the* R. *of the table.*)

MARIA. Curiously enough, I am able to control my excitement !

DUKE. Splendid !

RICHARD. Sing us something, Helen ! (*At* R. *side of the piano.*)

HELEN. I'm sorry, Richard, but I don't sing !

(RICHARD *moves up stage behind* HELEN *and goes up to the window.*)

Duke (*turning on his* r. *a little towards* Helen). I congratulate you; that is a great accomplishment! (*Returning to* Maria.) I suggest, my dear, our revered old friend Maria dances us the Charleston!

Maria. I'm neither your dear, or your revered, or your old friend; and I suggest you try and say something intelligent.

(Helen *commences to play, softly.*)

Duke (*pats her hand gently*). Naughty, naughty! that's the third time you have spoken harshly to me to-night!

Maria (*moving her hand*). Don't do that! I hate it! (*She moves a little* l.)

Duke (*moving up* r.c. *to* Helen's l. *Listening to her playing*). Exquisite! I feel rather in the mood to-night to engage a hundred lovely women, all with lovely voices, seated about on lovely divans, to sing to me in a whisper.

Maria (*returning and sitting in the chair* l. *of table*). If you had a little more brain you would be in an asylum!

(Richard, *up stage* c., *laughs rather loudly.*)

Duke (*looking round*). Richard has either enjoyed your joke immensely or has eaten something indigestible! Ho! Richard, tell them that story you told me at dinner! (*He gives a little to his* r.)

Richard (*nervously*). What story? (*Coming down from the window to the back of the table.*)

Duke. You know, the man who said he couldn't sing.

Richard. I don't remember it!

(Helen *stops playing and rises.*)

Duke. Don't be absurd! Of course you do!

(Helen *moves down to the back of the settee.*)

Richard. I tell you I don't!

Maria (*half turning in her chair towards* Richard). Do you tell coarse stories, Richard?

Richard. Certainly not! (*Turns quickly—facing her.*)

Maria. Then tell it!

Richard. Er—er—it has one word in it that I don't care to use before ladies!

Maria. Leave out the word.

Richard. Then the story has no point!

Duke (*returning to* r. *of* c.). Here, I'll tell it!

Richard. You'll do nothing of the sort.

Maria. Exactly! I thought so! (*To* Helen.) What I was saying to you just now—what does any woman know about any man?

DUKE. But what is much more to the point is, what does any man know about any woman ? (*He turns and moves to his* R.)

MARIA. Having made the remark of a complete imbecile, perhaps you will tell us the answer !

DUKE (*going to the front of the table*). He knows everything about them, and, you nasty old lady, you expected me to say he knew nothing about them ! Got you !

MARIA (*rising*). If you use the word " old " again to me, I'll throw something at you !

DUKE. Very well, but I pray that when I reach the age of nearly forty-one, I shall not be ashamed ! My stepmother, who will be forty-one in August, isn't !

MARIA. Beast ! (*Moves up* L. *of table—stops and turns.*) Beast ! (*She turns again and walks out of room into garden.*)

(RICHARD *follows her up, looking after her, and then comes to* L.C.)

DUKE (*moving to the settee and sitting at its* R. *end*). Got her that time !

RICHARD. George, you're a bounder ! (*Seats himself in the armchair* L. *of the table.*)

DUKE. Funny you should say that. A woman said exactly the same thing to me at dinner last night ! I suppose I am ! Am I a bounder, Helen ?

HELEN. I don't think so. (*She goes up* C.) But you have upset Maria terribly. (*She stands looking through the window.*)

RICHARD. And if you are a gentleman, you will at once go and tell her you are sorry !

DUKE. A gentleman, Richard, is a man of courage without imagination ! Were Maria a lady by nature instead of by birth, I should at once go and tell her I was sorry.

RICHARD (*rising and moving up* L. *of the table*). Then I shall go and tell her that I am sorry for you ! (*To* HELEN.) Will you forgive me ?

(*He goes out through the window. The* DUKE *watches him as he leaves and* HELEN *comes down to* R.C.)

DUKE. There's something terribly attractive about an English gentleman. (*Sighs.*) I wish I'd been born one instead of a duke.

HELEN (*laughing*). Why aren't you one ? (*She is standing at the head of the settee—looking down at him.*)

DUKE. It's out of the question ! If I were, the middle classes and the Americans visiting England would have nothing to talk about ! My mood to-night, Helen, is one of singular sadness ; I have a grievance against God's creatures ; I feel they don't appreciate me. Every morning of my life I expect to be wakened by someone saying " Come at once, you have been made Governor of the Bank of England," and the most that ever happens is someone says,

" There's a gent downstairs who says the President of the Divorce Court would like to speak to you ! "

HELEN. I think that is a great pity ! (*She sits on the settee beside him, L. end.*)

DUKE. It is, and it's expensive !

HELEN. Have you *no* ambition in life, *no* desire to do anything for anyone ?

DUKE. When I think of the miseries of others, my heart bleeds so profusely for them it almost ceases to bleed for the miseries of my own !

HELEN. Instead of only thinking about others, mightn't you be happier if you did something for them ?

DUKE. My dear ! the most that can be expected of any Duke is to think.

HELEN. Then has marriage no attraction for you ?

DUKE. It always has had considerable attraction for me ; no less than the husbands of three women I have known have threatened me with it !

HELEN. I was meaning some unmarried girl who was fond of you, and might make you very happy.

DUKE. Now it's very curious you should say that ; my trustees and myself meet in committee on that subject at eleven to-morrow morning !

HELEN. They want you to marry ?

DUKE. They insist !

HELEN (*rising*). Are you going to ?

DUKE. I have promised them an answer to-morrow at eleven.

HELEN (*turning on her L. hand, up to the piano, speaking as she moves to get cigarette-box*). What is your answer going to be ?

DUKE. I do not know !

HELEN (*returns to front of settee. Offers cigarette, standing above the DUKE*). Come and dine with me to-morrow evening and tell me what you have decided to do !

DUKE. I'd adore to ; (*takes a cigarette*) that's charming of you ; you're very sympathetic, Helen ! (*Sits up.*)

HELEN. I suppose it's because I like you.

DUKE. That's charming of you, really it is !

(RICHARD *enters through window* C. *and comes down to* L.C.)

RICHARD. George, I hope it amuses you to have made a woman cry !

(HELEN *turns up to piano, replacing box.*)

DUKE. But I have said nothing that could possibly make her cry !

RICHARD (L.C.). Didn't you in a sneering way accuse her of being forty-one ?

DUKE. I did! But she is not crying because I said she was forty-one; she's crying because she is forty-one!

RICHARD. Bounder!

HELEN (*crossing to him*). Is she very upset, Richard?

RICHARD. I hope I will never see anyone as upset as she is again; I could do nothing with her; she even asked me to tell her that story to take her mind off her unhappiness!

DUKE. Did she laugh?

RICHARD (*crossing* HELEN *to* R.C.). Laugh? It only increased her misery. I gathered the story was older than I was! (*Turns to* HELEN.) Oh, by the way, Tom Leggatt and his wife came in through the garden, they are with her now!

HELEN. Why don't they come in?

RICHARD. They don't want to. (*Turning to* DUKE.) Tom says he's content to see George in the "Tatler" or the "Sketch."

DUKE. I wonder why people dislike me so much?

RICHARD (*to him*). Because most times you're a damnable dislikeable feller, that's why.

DUKE. Do you know, I believe that's what it is! I'm almost sure it is!

HELEN (*smiles*). I don't think so. (*Moves up* L.) Why don't you both come and sit outside? I must go and talk to the Leggatts.

DUKE. If you don't mind, I think it would be wiser if we stayed here.

HELEN. Very well! (*She goes up to window.*) Help yourself, Richard, to a drink!

RICHARD. Many thanks! (*Follows up* C. *Then moves down* L. *of table.*)

(HELEN *exits through the window.*)

(*At the word* "drink" DUKE *goes up to table.*)

DUKE (R. *of table*). Water or soda?

RICHARD (L.C.). I won't have a drink, thanks. Tom Leggatt has been telling me there's a rumour all over the city that you are broke!

DUKE. The city for once is correct! To-morrow morning at eleven o'clock I have to decide which it's to be, marriage or bankruptcy. (*Pours whisky.*)

RICHARD. I'm sorry, very sorry! (*Sits in chair* L. *of table.*)

DUKE. I'm touched, Richard!

RICHARD. But you couldn't have got through everything.

DUKE (*he puts soda into his glass*). I am given to understand that I have even eaten the grass my horses live on! (*Drinks.*)

RICHARD. I am sorry!

DUKE. Thank you, Richard. (*Moves down a little* R. *of* C.). And at eleven to-morrow, I, George, twelfth Duke of Bristol, a man whose very soul quivers with sentiment, whose heart beats only for romance, has to sell himself for money! (*Drinks.*) It's a very serious thing, Richard.

RICHARD. I agree it is!

DUKE (*advancing to him a little*). But you don't know how serious it is! It means infidelity, Richard, that's what it means—infidelity!

RICHARD. It might not; I *have* known cases!

DUKE. For her sake, it's good for you to be an optimist, but you're wrong. I am a man who should essentially marry for love!

RICHARD. We all should.

DUKE. Lying in bed in the morning, how often have I pictured myself walking down a beautiful lane, and there at the bottom is a railway crossing, and with her heel caught in the line I see the divine woman of the world; in the distance I hear an express train! I dash, I seize her in my arms—and as the train passes us, I realize I have saved her! Wiping the blood from my eyes—you will notice although I have saved her, I did not come out of it unscathed myself——

RICHARD. I noticed it—it was a charming touch!

DUKE. I realize that I have met my divinity, from whom I will never again be parted.

RICHARD. Most attractive! Most attractive!

DUKE (*moving* R.). But—my financial position is such that I dare not even go near a railway station. (*Sits on the settee.*)

RICHARD (*rising and crossing to him*). I sympathize with you very deeply, believe me, I do!

DUKE. As much as you are able to, I am sure you do! but to really understand is to be able to love as I could! (*He looks in the direction of the window.*)

RICHARD. I too have loved!

DUKE. *Quite so*, but if you don't mind, I would like to restrict this discussion to ladies!

RICHARD. And those are the only ones I have ever loved, and not ladies—lady. I have loved for over twenty years the most beautiful lady in all the world.

DUKE. Why haven't you told me about this?

RICHARD. One doesn't wear one's heart on one's sleeve!

DUKE. But one should! What's the fun if one doesn't?

RICHARD. A love like mine cannot be discussed! (*He moves a little to his* L.)

DUKE. Do I know her?

RICHARD. Intimately.

DUKE. Who is it?—Who is it?

RICHARD (*turns—pauses—looks up stage—then speaks*). Maria Wislack!

DUKE (*rising from settee—indignantly*). Richard, when I told you the tragedy of my life, the depth of my feelings, I did not for a moment believe you would treat it with levity—make jokes about it!

RICHARD. I'm not. I tell you I have loved her for more than twenty years!

DUKE (*angrily; moving to him*). Do you mean to tell me that you have loved that old——

RICHARD. Silence! If I am not mistaken you were about to call her by a name that would have prevented me ever speaking to you again!

DUKE. Have a drink—or have you had too many?

RICHARD. I will have a drink; (*moving a little to* L.) and 1 have not had too many!

DUKE (*going up to the table, pours out a drink, which he brings to* RICHARD). Richard, old boy, I love you as a brother, but I must say it, I'd rather see you dead!

RICHARD. George, I mean it! If you say one word again that reflects in the least way against Maria, Mrs. Wislack, our friendship is at an end.

DUKE. Very well, but you can't stop me wishing you were dead!

(RICHARD *moves farther* L.)

Did you know her late husband, Arthur Wislack?

RICHARD. Did I know him? Did I watch him with murder in my heart, treating that divine creature with cruelty, neglect—and eventually die of drink?

DUKE (L.C.). He hated drink!

RICHARD (L.). Then why did he?

DUKE. He chose it as being the most agreeable way of being unconscious whilst waiting for his release.

RICHARD (*moves angrily up stage* L., *putting his glass on the table*). I warned you, George, I told you if you said another word that reflected——

DUKE (*moving* R. *of table*). Sit down and don't be so damned dignified. Besides, you haven't finished your drink! (*He turns away and goes over to the small table below the door* R.)

RICHARD (*at back of table* C.). On that account only will I speak to you again.

DUKE (*picks up cigar-box and crosses to* R. *of table* C.). Have a cigar?

RICHARD. If you are apologizing to me, George, I should prefer it in the form of one of your own cigars!

DUKE. Richard, if I have in any way hurt your feelings, I apologize. Now will you stop sulking and have a cigar?

RICHARD. Thank you. (*Takes one and moves* L.)

DUKE. Does she love you? (*Puts cigar-box back after taking one himself.*)

RICHARD (*at the fireplace* L.). How should I know ?

DUKE (*by table* R., *lighting cigar*). But haven't you asked her if she does ?

RICHARD. Mrs. Wislack's income is at the least twenty-five thousand pounds a year, mine is three hundred ! (*Lights cigar.*)

DUKE. With or without income tax ?

RICHARD. I'm not a fool, George.

DUKE (*coming to* c.). But I was always under the impression that you had at least fifteen hundred a year !

RICHARD (*moving down* L.). Yes, but unfortunately, all the horses I have been interested in have been entirely without ambition —they only run for running's sake !

DUKE. We have a great deal in common. But I take everything back ; you have offered me a reason why you are right to love her. I applaud you ! (*Moves to chair* L. *of table.*)

RICHARD. What do you mean ?

DUKE. She has twenty-five thousand a year ! (*He sits in chair* L. *of table.*)

RICHARD. Are you suggesting that the reason I love her is because she has money ?

DUKE. I suggest it's the reason you should !

RICHARD. George, let us understand each other ; my love for Maria has lasted through the years ; I love her, not for what she has, but for what she is. If she were poor I'd ask her to marry me to-night.

DUKE. I had no idea you loved her as much as this, Richard.

RICHARD. Well, I hope you understand it now !

DUKE. I do, and I propose to help you !

RICHARD. How ?

DUKE. I shall go to her at once, with a tremor in my voice, I will tell her of your love for her !

RICHARD. And then ?

DUKE. I will wait for the answer and bring it back to you !

RICHARD. Thank you, but if there is to be any tremoring of the voice, I will be obliged if you will leave it to me !

DUKE. And to-night !

RICHARD. What do you mean ?

DUKE. I am determined before the night is out that you will be under the impression that you are the happiest man in the world !

RICHARD. How do you propose to do that ?

DUKE. You shall tell her here in this room of your love for her !

RICHARD. It's out of the question.

DUKE. I insist !

RICHARD. I haven't the courage !

DUKE (*looks at whisky*). You shall have it !

RICHARD. My dear George, hundreds of times I have been on the

verge of asking her, and my courage has failed me at the last moment.
(*He sits on the pouffe* L.)

Duke. Ever tried brandy ?

Richard. I have !

Duke. No good ?

Richard. One night I sat with a bottle of brandy in front of
me, and I recited to it the language I would use when asking her to
be my wife, with the result that when I entered the room I was
unable to even wish her good evening.

Duke. Bad luck !

Richard. No, no, I'm resigned to bachelorhood and solitude !
Don't encourage me, there's a good fellow, it's hopeless.

Duke (*rising and going to him*). Richard, I give you my word of
honour that a month from to-night you'll pop into her bed and say :
" Maria, here I am ! "

Richard (*rising*). George, that is an observation which I consider most *un*suitable here *or* in the place that you suggest I should
make it !

Duke. I was speaking metaphorically !

Richard. I trust so !

Duke (*putting his arm on* Richard's *shoulder*). Loving her as you
do, Richard, you must think what it would mean to you ; someone
to talk to, to be with, no money cares, no cares of any kind, just a
happy, jolly fellow smiling his way through life !

Richard. Attractive—(*shaking his head*) but it's not for me.

Duke (*appealingly*). Think of the little ones prattling up and
down the room—no, no, I take that back !

Richard. Why ?

Duke. Very well, if you insist. (*Moves away a little towards* C.)

Richard. Married life without children to me——

(Duke *makes noise trying to stop himself laughing, and moves to* R.)

Are you laughing, George ?

Duke (*turns*). Laughing ? I have a cold coming on !

Richard. It's the sort of thing you would laugh at !

Duke. Not as much as the children would, Richard !

Richard. What do you mean by that ? (*He re-seats himself on
the pouffe.*)

Duke (*checking himself and going up* R.C. *to the window*). Nothing !
(*Turning down* C.) Listen, I'm going to help you ; (*coming to*
Richard's R. *hand*) when she comes into this room, I'm going to
force myself to be nice to her, I am going to be at my best ; I'm, as it
were, going to warm her up for you, to make your proposal, Richard ;
at the right moment I will persuade Helen to accompany me to
the garden, thereby leaving her alone with you, and all that you
will have to do will be to put the question !

Richard (*jumping up*). No, no !

DUKE. I insist! (*Putting* RICHARD *down again.*)

RICHARD. No, no!

DUKE. Richard, either you or I will ask her to marry you to-night!

RICHARD. How—how—would you advise me to begin?

DUKE (*moving* C.). Well, I have always found it wiser to begin by putting both your arms round them, pausing for a second before speaking, and then saying, " God, how I love you! "

RICHARD. Yes, that might be a good plan with women that are married, but would it be with a woman that you want to!

DUKE. True! There you've got me! Let me think—yes! I think it would be; women love surprises.

RICHARD. She's had too many! And, if it misfired, she's as strong as a horse!

DUKE (*to him again*). Then I should treat her softly; I should metaphorically coo at her!

RICHARD (*shakes his head*). No! I don't think so!

DUKE. Why not?

RICHARD. She's clever; she would metaphorically coo back!

DUKE. Then you must rely on instinct!

RICHARD (*rising*). No, no, I can't! She would think I wanted to marry her for her money!

DUKE. Nonsense! She is much too vain! I insist, Richard. Understand?

(HELEN *laughs off* R.)

'Ssh!

RICHARD. I'll try; but you will be nice to her, George?

DUKE. Even you won't know me. Richard, rely on me, I am going to pave the way for you marvellously! (*He moves up a little* L.)

(MARIA *enters by the window, followed by* HELEN. *The former looks at* RICHARD, *then at the* DUKE, *and comes to the* R. *of the table.*)

HELEN (*in the window*). You *should* have come out; it's a divine night! (*She comes down to the back of the table.*)

DUKE. Had you and Maria been alone, we should have!

MARIA (*holding up the decanter*). You seem to have drunk quite a nice lot of this!

DUKE. I'm afraid I did that; Richard let me down; he finds one whisky and soda in the evening is enough!

MARIA. I'm glad to hear it! (*Puts decanter down and comes to* L. *end of settee.*)

DUKE (*moving over to her in front of the table*). Maria!

(RICHARD *follows to about* C.)

MARIA. Well?

DUKE. I apparently said something to-night, quite unintention-ally, that offended and hurt you ?

MARIA. Well ?

DUKE. I'm sorry !

MARIA. Obviously you have been drinking !

DUKE. What makes you say that ?

MARIA. You would never have apologized if you hadn't ! (*She sits on the settee.*)

DUKE (R.C.). You're wrong. I drank because I was depressed. Richard depressed me !

MARIA. Ho !

(HELEN *watches this scene from the back.*)

DUKE. Whilst you were in the garden, Richard has been pointing to me my limitations, so gently, so understandingly, that I was compelled to listen ; he has made me feel that all is not well with George, the twelfth Duke of Bristol !

(RICHARD *moves nearer to him.*)

MARIA. Ho !

(HELEN *moves round* L. *of the table and sits on the pouffe.*)

DUKE. The simplicity of his nature conquered me. I thought I had known Richard all my life. I was wrong—I did not know him until to-night. (*Pats him on the shoulder.*) Dear Richard !

MARIA. Ho !

DUKE. You haven't lost your voice, by any chance, have you ?

MARIA. No. Why ?

DUKE. It's unlike you to be only able to say " Ho ! "

MARIA. I'm interested ! I'm listening ! Tell us what he told you.

DUKE. It wasn't so much what he told me about myself as what he told me about himself that affected me !

MARIA. As for instance ?

DUKE. His gentleness and kindly feeling towards the world, his love of only that which is beautiful, his adoration for little children !

MARIA. How many has he ?

DUKE. Richard is a bachelor.

MARIA. That hasn't answered my question !

DUKE. None !

MARIA. How do you know ?

DUKE (*looking at* RICHARD). He is not that kind of man !

MARIA (*also looking at* RICHARD). I see. Go on !

DUKE. That—in effect—is all !

MARIA. Do you ask me to believe that in listening to that ridiculous nonsense you have become a better man ?

DUKE. I have a feeling that to-morrow morning I shall find

B

myself standing side by side with the most upright man that England has produced.

MARIA. I trust that to-morrow morning you will wake with a very bad headache and no recollection of the nonsense you have been talking to me to-night!

DUKE. Very well, I shall say no more!

HELEN. Oh, please do, I'm terribly interested.

DUKE (*crossing in front of* RICHARD *to* HELEN *and taking her hand*). Helen, my dear, you and I are only very young——

MARIA. What?

DUKE. Perhaps we are right to believe all that is told us, but, (*turns to* RICHARD) if Richard has lied to me to-night and has cheated me into believing he is all the things that the suggestion is that he is not, I will never speak to him again!

RICHARD. I said nothing I did not mean!

DUKE. And I believe you, Richard, and through you, I have a feeling to-night, (*crosses him to* R.C.) and for the first time in my life, that I would like to get nearer to nature; I would like to walk on grass,

(RICHARD *sits in the chair* L. *of table*)

inhale—(*he turns up towards the window during this*) the scent of flowers, listen to the birds singing their simple songs of love! (*Turns to* MARIA *and turns away again.*) I feel it would help me to find myself more completely.

MARIA. Try the morning, birds don't sing at night.

DUKE. Not for you. Helen, would it amuse you to accompany me?

HELEN (*rising*). I'd love to! (*She joins the* DUKE *in the window.*)

DUKE. I'm delighted. You will find me very silent!

HELEN. I don't mind!

(*They exeunt through the window.*)

MARIA. Well?

(RICHARD *smiles at her nervously.*)

Don't you wish to hear the birds singing their simple songs of love!

RICHARD. I rather felt he was exaggerating!

MARIA. Is that young man drunk, or has he acquired a habit of borrowing money from women?

RICHARD. Er—I don't quite understand!

MARIA. I don't know what's the matter with him because I know he hates me!

RICHARD. I think you are wrong. He said only charming things about you when you were outside.

MARIA. Tell me one!

RICHARD (*hesitating*). He said you had a heart of gold!

MARIA. I knew he hated me!

RICHARD. Not at all! And many other equally nice things!

MARIA. Tell me some of those lofty thoughts which have made him wish to walk on grass.

RICHARD. It was nothing really; I was describing to him the loneliness of one's life, living alone, no one to talk to, no one to care for, the utter misery of it all! and the need men have for the affection of a good woman!

MARIA. Go on!

RICHARD. It would bore you!

MARIA. Not at all.

RICHARD. Thank you! I drew a little picture of returning to one's home in the evening——

MARIA. Where had you been in the afternoon?

RICHARD. Nowhere in particular!

MARIA. I see. Go on.

RICHARD. And there seated at one's dinner table, a divine lady who——

MARIA. To whom you would pass a few pleasant words on your way upstairs to dress to go out to dinner with someone else.

RICHARD. Not at all. I should stay and dine with her!

MARIA. Unusual but interesting. Go on!

RICHARD. I described to him the happiness one would feel in having someone one loved to dine with and talk to instead of sitting down miserably eating one's food as I do, alone.

MARIA. Horrid for you! Feeling as you do, Richard, I wonder you don't marry?

RICHARD. Ah! (*He sighs.*)

MARIA. Meaning——?

RICHARD. The love of a good woman is not for me!

MARIA. Then try one of the others; there are any number of those to choose from.

RICHARD. No, no! (*He rises and moves across the room in front of the settee to* R.) There is and only has been one woman that I would care to share my life with. (*He remains below the* R. *end of the settee, half turned from* MARIA.)

MARIA. And have you asked her to?

RICHARD. No.

MARIA. Why?

RICHARD. She is too good, too beautiful, too noble, for such as me.

MARIA. If she is as you describe her, I agree! But she may not be quite all those things.

RICHARD. To me she is!

MARIA. Tell me more about her! Come and sit down.

(*He hesitates.*)

Come along. Come along. (*Pats seat beside her.*)

RICHARD (*sitting on her* R. *hand*). No ! I must for ever love her from a distance ; I must for ever worship her in silence ; I——

MARIA. Oh, shut up !

RICHARD. I'm sorry !

MARIA. How much longer are you going on beating about the bush instead of coming out in the open like a man and saying, " Maria, I love you. Will you or won't you be my wife " ?

RICHARD. How did you know ?

MARIA. How did I know ? Haven't I had to listen to this meandering rubbish every time I ever met you ?

RICHARD. And I had no idea you knew !

MARIA. You love me ?

RICHARD. With all my heart, with all——

MARIA. Quite so, but let us proceed ! Is your object matrimony or the other ?

RICHARD. I would give ten years of my life to be your husband.

MARIA. I have no desire that our marriage ceremony should take the form of a burial service. Now, Richard, I should like you to know that I am very fond of you !

RICHARD. I cannot believe it ! Why should you care for me ?

MARIA. You would be wise in encouraging me not to dwell on that.

RICHARD. Quite.

MARIA. And in addition you are the only man I know that I would for a moment consider marrying !

RICHARD. This is too wonderful to be true !

MARIA. Don't be too excited, you're getting the best part first ! You agree, to be a successful business man you must be practical.

RICHARD. Most emphatically I do.

MARIA. Very well ! So let us be practical ! My income is twenty-five thousand pounds a year !

RICHARD. Many congratulations !

MARIA. Thank you ! What is yours ?

RICHARD. Mine ?

MARIA. Yes.

RICHARD. Well, it varies ; sometimes it's up, and then again it's down !

MARIA. How much is it when it's up ?

RICHARD. Do you know, money means so little to me, I haven't really an idea !

MARIA. Where do you bank ?

RICHARD. Anywhere—I simply don't care.

MARIA. Could you provide for me ?

RICHARD. I *could*, but I'm not sure it would be in the way that you have been used to !

MARIA. Well, I could provide for both of us in the way that I have been used to.

RICHARD. That is true.

MARIA. So the money is of no consequence ?

RICHARD. No.

MARIA. The only question is, would we be happy ?

RICHARD. I should be very happy.

MARIA. As I am going to do the providing, would you mind including me in your conversation ? I said would we, meaning myself, be happy ?

RICHARD. My life would be devoted to nothing else ! You have known me long enough surely to know that ?

MARIA. Having been married before, I know that it is possible that you are none of the things you appear to be !

RICHARD. I am described by my friends as a simple fellow !

MARIA. So was my late husband ! He was so simple that I never understood one single thing he did for eighteen years. Richard, you said that you love me ?

RICHARD. With all my heart, with all——

MARIA. " I love you " embraces all that. Now, I have a house in Scotland—what is to-day ?

RICHARD. Tuesday.

MARIA. Tuesday—it is ? Yes, Tuesday ! Very well, I suggest that you and I on Thursday night by the midnight train travel there for one month !

RICHARD. It sounds delightful, but with what particular object ?

MARIA. To all intents and purposes we will spend a month alone together as married people.

RICHARD (*rising*). You and I spend a month alone together as married people !

MARIA. Yes.

RICHARD. You're not serious ?

MARIA. I am !

RICHARD. But what an extraordinary good idea. What an intensely good idea.

MARIA. I'm glad you like it. We will, so to speak, breakfast, lunch and dine together, just as if we were married.

RICHARD (*moving to* c.). But this is perfectly delightful ! I really congratulate you most sincerely ! Charming ! and the courage of it ! (*Returning on her* L.)

MARIA. If at the end of the month I find that we think alike as it were, that you are a pleasant person to live with, I'll marry you.

RICHARD. And if I'm not, we will have had a grand time, and no harm done.

MARIA. None.

RICHARD (*moving to* c.). Really, I can't tell you how highly I think of it ! It's daring without being unattractive, it's attractive, with no loss of beauty, it's wise without being cunning ! (*Returning and standing above the* L. *arm of the settee.*) Really, I do congratulate you! I never remember looking forward to anything so much! And the courage of it! (*He comes round the arm of the settee; she moves a little and he sits on her* L. *hand. There is a momentary pause, during which he looks at her.*) Ho! if there were only more women in the world like you, what a happy world the world would be!

MARIA. Finished?

RICHARD. Not at all! I could go on for hours! I wish I could decide whether the wisdom or the courage of it appeals to me more.

MARIA. Finished?

RICHARD. Only for the moment. I'm so struck by the whole idea I have not been able to half express myself.

MARIA. Each night you will hear a clock in the hall strike eleven——

RICHARD. Now that's original. Really, I must congratulate you again.

MARIA. ——which will be the signal for you to start putting your coat on!

RICHARD. With what idea?

MARIA. With the idea of going out.

RICHARD. But I shall have had all the exercise I· need in the day! Oh, I know, the dog!

MARIA. On the hall table you will find a lantern, it will help you to find your way to the hotel a mile away!

RICHARD. Precisely for what reason do I go to the hotel?

MARIA. It's optional, but it's the place where you will be sleeping.

RICHARD (*rising and turning a little to* C.). Ho! So I don't sleep in the house?

MARIA. You don't!

RICHARD (*turning*). Ho! how about wet nights?

MARIA. I should advise your bringing a raincoat.

RICHARD. Yes—raincoat! I must say it seems to me you would learn a great deal more about me if I were actually in the house the whole time!

MARIA. I shall endeavour to learn all I want to know without that.

RICHARD. Very well, but——

MARIA. And I am not in the habit of staying in houses with a man alone.

RICHARD. I trust I am a gentleman.

MARIA. I shall be able to tell in a month's time. Well, what do you say? (*She rises.*)

RICHARD. I accept, of course! And I wish you to know I shall do everything in my power to prove to you that your happiness with me is assured!

(*Both in front of settee, standing.*)

MARIA. I don't want you to do anything—I just want you to be natural.

RICHARD. I could not be anything else !

MARIA. Then we leave midnight Thursday. (*She crosses him to* C.)

RICHARD. We do !

MARIA. You will call for me and take me to the station ?

RICHARD. I will.

MARIA. Very well. (*She looks up* L.) My cloak, Richard.

RICHARD. You're going ? (*He moves at the back of the table to chair up stage* L. *for cloak.*)

MARIA. Yes ! I had no idea it was so late.

(*He comes* C. *and helps her with her cloak, standing on her* L.)

I make it a rule, Richard, never to be out of my bed after 11.30.

RICHARD. I shall be very happy to acquire a similar habit ! I'll see you home.

MARIA. It's not necessary. I'll go through the garden. My house is only twenty yards away ! Good night, Richard.

(*She offers her cheek for him to kiss. He hesitates, then kisses her.*)

I hope I shall find that you are all that I think you are !

RICHARD. I hope you will find that I am a great deal more than you think I am.

(*She goes up* R. *of table and stops.*)

MARIA. Good night.

RICHARD (*moving across to up* R.C.). Good night, darling !

(*She exits through the window into garden to* R.)

(*He goes up and looks after her happily and then he helps himself to a whisky and soda.* R. *of table.*)

(DUKE *enters* C. *from* L.)

DUKE (*speaking from the window*). Do I, or do I not, see a happy man ?

RICHARD (*drinking*). You do.

DUKE (*coming to the back of table,* L. *end*). She's accepted you ?

RICHARD. She hasn't. (*Puts down glass.*)

DUKE. She's refused you and you're delighted—and so am I !

RICHARD. She has not refused me.

DUKE. Well, what did she do ?

RICHARD. That is entirely my business ! (*Moves down* R.)

(HELEN *enters* C. *from* L. *and comes to* R. *of table. The* DUKE *moves to* L. *of table.*)

HELEN. Maria has gone away in a terribly good mood, Richard. Am I to congratulate you ?

RICHARD (R.C.). In a way, Helen dear, at all events you will be able to ! A month from to-day you will look at me and say " There's a happy man of the world ! "

DUKE. Then you are engaged to her ?

RICHARD. I tell you I'm not.

DUKE. Then what are you ?

RICHARD. Well, I'm half engaged to her, and half married to her !

DUKE. Has the old lady been trying to find out what effect drink has on you ? (*Sits in chair* L. *of table.*)

RICHARD (*advancing a step*). Unless you are able to speak of my future wife in prettier language I shall ask you not to speak to me again.

HELEN (*with a slight movement towards* RICHARD). Why a month from to-day, Richard ?

RICHARD. The position is this : owing to their being men in the world like George, we are in consequence all suspects ! I leave on Thursday night for Scotland with Maria, that we may spend a month together with the idea of discovering if we possess those things in common that would make for permanent happy married life !

DUKE. You and she go off to Scotland for a month alone to find out if you will be all right married ?

RICHARD (*crossing to him*). I dislike your phraseology, but the answer is, we do !

(HELEN *moves to behind settee.*)

DUKE. Very hot !

RICHARD. What do you mean ?

DUKE. Well, isn't it ?

RICHARD. I can now see why Maria mistrusts all men !

DUKE. But, damn it, you can't say it's too good going away for a whole month with a woman !

RICHARD. We will, if you don't mind, in future refer to her as lady. (*He moves to the* R., *hesitates and returns to the* DUKE.) You are not suggesting that I would stay in the same house with her at night alone, are you ?

DUKE. Aren't you ?

RICHARD. How dare you ! Only a man like you could have ever thought of such a thing. I sleep at the hotel.

DUKE. You mean to tell me that every night you leave her and go to an hotel ?

RICHARD. What else do you suggest I should do ?

DUKE. Stay in the house with her.

RICHARD. You cad !

DUKE (*with a quick thought*). Suppose it's raining !

RICHARD. I have thought of that. I am taking a raincoat.

(HELEN *turns to the piano.*)

DUKE (*looking at* HELEN). What do you think about it ?

HELEN. To me it all seems very unnecessary. Nothing would induce me to go to Scotland at this time of year. If I cared for anyone enough, I should know him so well I'd marry him at once ! (*She sits on the piano stool.*)

DUKE. I agree !

(HELEN *commences to play.*)

RICHARD (C.). I'm sorry, but I see Maria's point perfectly ; I think she is perfectly right.

DUKE. Do you think you will be able to convince her you are all right, Richard ?

RICHARD. I am all right.

DUKE. Good ! I wish I were there to help you ! One minute !

RICHARD. Anything the matter ?

DUKE. An idea is creeping into my brain ! Richard, I am going to be of infinite service to you !

RICHARD. How ?

DUKE. Every night you return to that hotel you will find me there prepared with what you have to say to her to-morrow !

RICHARD. What do you mean ?

DUKE. My position in London is precarious. I wish to leave it ; it is suggested I should make up my mind on a subject of considerable finality immediately. I do not wish to ; it would suit me perfectly to spend a quiet month in Scotland !

(HELEN *ceases playing.*)

RICHARD. And come and stay at my hotel ?

DUKE. Precisely.

RICHARD. That would be marvellous. No ! No !

DUKE. Why not ?

RICHARD. If Maria knew she would strongly disapprove.

DUKE. She wouldn't know. I would enter my name in the hotel book as Smith ! Only my manner and my appearance would suggest I am who I am.

RICHARD. I like the idea, but I must think about it.

DUKE (*rising*). It's settled, Richard, I am coming. I leave by the midnight train on Friday !

RICHARD. No, no ! It must be talked over very seriously.

DUKE. It shall be ! (*Crossing him to* R.) Have you any whisky in your rooms ?

RICHARD. I think so.

DUKE. We will adjourn there ! (*He turns up stage on the* R. *of the settee to* HELEN.) Helen, I dine with you to-morrow--I look forward to it very much.

HELEN. Nine o'clock.

DUKE. To the minute. And thank you for an exceedingly pleasant evening. Good night. (*He goes out door* R.)

HELEN. Good night.

RICHARD (*going up* C. *towards* HELEN). Good night, Helen dear ! I can't tell you how happy I am !

HELEN (*rising and meeting him up stage* R. *of* C.). I hope you always will be, Richard.

RICHARD. I know I shall.

DUKE (*from off* R.). Come on, Richard. Good night, Helen.

RICHARD (*shaking hands with* HELEN *and crossing her to* R.). Good night. (*He exits after the* DUKE.)

(HELEN *remains for a moment thinking. Then suddenly passes at the back of the table to the telephone.*)

HELEN. Mayfair 1062. (*Looks towards the door* R. *Pause.*) Is that Mrs. Portious' house ? Would you be good enough to tell Mrs. Portious that Miss Hayle will be unable to dine with her on Friday night as she is going to Scotland——? Thank you.

CURTAIN.

ACT II

SCENE.—MRS. WISLACK'S *house in Scotland.*

TIME.—*Three weeks later.*

The table L.C. *is set for one person.*
HELEN *is discovered seated in the chair on the* R. *of the fireplace, reading.*

(MARIA *enters from the* L.)

MARIA (*looking at the clock* L.C.). Twenty minutes to two! Hasn't that young man you like so much come in yet? (*She moves across to the door up stage* R.C.)

HELEN. No!

MARIA. Does he realize those beasts of servants left me at a moment's notice, and we are doing all their work? (*Returns to the front of table* L.C.)

HELEN. Of course!

MARIA. Well, why isn't he here for his lunch at one o'clock, as you asked him to be? (*Picks up "Tatler."*)

HELEN. I'm nervous that something has happened to him.

MARIA. Nervous that something hasn't! (*Crosses to the settee* R.) The way you pander to this man, Helen, makes me ill with rage! (*She sits on the settee.*)

(HELEN *smiles.*)

HELEN. I'm sorry, darling!

MARIA. You follow him here! You persuade me to let him stay here—you wait on him hand and foot—ho! You make me so angry—I can't speak!

HELEN (*laughs*). I'm sorry!

MARIA. There's nothing to be amused about. Having spent three weeks with him practically alone, haven't you discovered that he's one of the most odious creatures that ever lived?

HELEN. The only thing that I've discovered is that I'm the happiest woman in the world! (*She rises, and turning round her chair to the* R. *goes to the small table* R. *of the fireplace.*)

MARIA. You don't mean to tell me you still like him?

HELEN. I have *never* been so happy, darling! (*Taking a jewel-case off the table* R.C. *with her back to* MARIA.)

27

MARIA. God give me strength! How can you tolerate his unutterable selfishness?

HELEN. Easily! (*She comes down* R.C. *to* MARIA.) It's only part of his education. But one of the only things the Duke of Bristol is unconscious of is his selfishness.

MARIA. And realizing that, you still like him? Terrible! terrible!

(HELEN *gives* MARIA *small box.*)

What's this?

HELEN. A present for you, darling. An appreciation of my gratitude to you. I telegraphed to London for it the second day I was here.

MARIA. But for what? (*Opening box.*)

HELEN. For being the cause of my spending three weeks practically alone with dear George. (*She sits on the settee above* MARIA.)

MARIA. It's sweet of you, Helen dear, and I adore it; and all that I can say is, I hope you will always be as happy as you appear to be now. (*She kisses* HELEN.)

HELEN. Thanks to *you*, darling, I'm going to be. (*She rises as she speaks and goes to the table* L.C. *and takes a cigarette from box.*)

MARIA. I take it he has asked you to marry him?

HELEN. Not yet, but he's soon going to. (*Goes up* C., *lighting her cigarette, and moves towards door up* R.)

MARIA. I hope you'll be happy. (*Looks at the clock again.*) Richard has been a long time gone to the village?

HELEN (*at door up* R.C.). The hill back from the village is steep and three miles long—and owing to your servants leaving you, and the car not being available till this afternoon, he has had to climb it twice to-day.

MARIA. But he left here before twelve.

HELEN. It's a steep hill, darling, and three miles long. (*She moves down at the back of the settee.*)

MARIA. You'd find excuses for anyone! (*Puts down paper.*) Helen, as a friend, what is your true opinion of Richard?

HELEN (*sitting on the down-stage arm of the settee*). I'm sure that Richard is the kindest, sweetest man I have ever known.

MARIA. That's what he appears to be. Do you think it's genuine?

HELEN. What do you mean?

MARIA. You don't think he's merely giving a good impression?

HELEN. No, I'm sure he's not! But if he is, darling, he's an unusually clever man.

MARIA. In what way?

HELEN. You haven't left *much* undone to find out if he has any particular weakness, have you, darling?

MARIA. How can you be so horrid! I've never been as nice to

anyone as I've been to Richard. Are you suggesting that I haven't been nice to him ?

HELEN. No ; how could I suggest such a thing, when Richard described you as an angel !

MARIA. When did he ?

HELEN. Last night, this morning, always when he speaks of you.

MARIA. Yes, but perhaps he said it hoping you'd repeat it.

(HELEN *looks at her.*)

HELEN. You must have discovered very little about Richard to even *think* that, darling.

MARIA. Anyway, I'm glad he said it, very glad.

(*The* DUKE *is heard off* R. *whistling, coming nearer.*)

(HELEN *smiles and goes up to the* R. *of the porch door.*)

HELEN. Here's George. Isn't it divine to hear him so happy ?

(*The* DUKE *enters from the porch* R. *and comes above the settee to* R.C.)

DUKE. Tell me something more exquisite than Scotland on a beautiful day ?

MARIA. You !

(DUKE *moves down* L.C.)

HELEN (*moving above settee to* R.C.). Thank God ! nothing has *happened* to you, George !

DUKE. Why, did you think something had ? (*He comes to her* L.)

HELEN (*above settee* R.C.). I did rather. As you went out I asked you, as there were no servants, to be in to lunch at *one*, and when quarter to two came, I began to think that something *terrible* had happened to you—(*pause*)—as you knew we had no servants.

DUKE. Charming ! Charming ! I'm grateful !

(*He hands* HELEN *hat and stick, which she hangs in the porch* R.)

The fact of the matter is, I lost myself in a letter I was writing to the " Morning Post " on " Why England always loses at games." After lunch I will read it to you. (*He turns to* C.)

HELEN (*up* R.C.). That will be divine !

DUKE (*to* MARIA). I think it will cause a sensation !

MARIA. That you can write a letter at all will cause a great sensation !

(*The* DUKE *looks at her and turns to* L.)

DUKE. Writing it has quite exhausted me. Is lunch ready ? I feel quite hungry ! (*He goes round the* L. *end of the table* L.C. *to the back of it.*)

MARIA. Lunch has been ready for three-quarters of an hour!

DUKE. No! I hope it isn't spoilt. (*Sits in the chair at the back of the table.*)

MARIA (*to* HELEN). He—he—hopes it isn't—— (*Unable to speak any further.*)

HELEN. I'll bring it to you, George dear.

(HELEN *goes out by the door* R. *below the porch.*)

DUKE. And what have *you* been doing, Maria dear? (*Shaking out serviette.*)

MARIA. Don't be so damn patronizing! I have been cleaning up your filthy untidy bedroom, and cooking your lunch.

DUKE. Ha! But if you hadn't quarrelled with your servants you wouldn't have had to do either!

MARIA (*angrily*). I did not quarrel with my servants!

DUKE. Then they quarrelled with you—which is a mere dis-tinction without a difference.

MARIA (*rises and crosses to* R. *of table*). George!

DUKE. Yes, Maria dear?

MARIA. Look at me. Does my face at this moment express anything to you?

DUKE. No.

MARIA. Well, there is a hand at my side imploring me to let it smack your stupid face!

DUKE. I forgive you, because I realize either through their or your fault you have lost your servants, and you are tired.

MARIA (*moving to* R.). Oh, Heaven, help me to remain something of a lady! (*Sits on the up-stage arm of the settee.*)

(HELEN *re-enters* R. *and moving straight across below the table, goes round its* L. *end and places a plate in front of the* DUKE.)

HELEN. There, George dear!

DUKE (*smiling at her*). Thank you, Helen. Some bread?

HELEN. I'm so sorry!

(*She hurries back to the door* R. *and goes out again.*)

DUKE. By the way, where is Richard?

MARIA. Richard at this moment is walking up that hill with things that you will eat for your dinner to-night.

DUKE. Good.

MARIA. Good.

DUKE. I hope he hasn't forgotten to bring me my " Times."

MARIA (*looks at him*). You hope he——

(HELEN *re-enters, carrying a plate with bread; she crosses to the* DUKE *as before.*)

HELEN. Bread, George darling.

Duke. And some butter, dear!

(Helen *again goes back and exits quickly.*)

Maria (*rising and walking to him* R. *of the table*). In the cellar there is champagne, Moselle, hock, claret—please let me fetch you something?

Duke. Maria, you know I never drink at lunch!

Maria. But I want you to. I want you to let me fetch it for you!

Duke. If you will allow me to say so, your joke is singularly unfunny.

(Maria *moves down* R.)

(Helen *enters again holding a plate in each hand; she comes to the*
R. *of the table.*)

Helen. Butter, George? (*She puts the butter on his* R. *hand, and comes round to his* L. *and shows him pudding.*) You would like some rice pudding?

Duke. To say I would like rice pudding, Helen, would be as inaccurate as it would be insincere—but to say that I am hungry and will have some rice pudding is an entirely different matter! Where's the cream?

Helen. There is no cream.

Duke. What!

Maria (*crossing to him at the* R. *end of the table*). Do you know what would give me more pleasure than anything else in the world?

Duke. I cannot imagine.

Maria. To rub your nose in rice pudding!

Duke. Even if it is through one's own fault one is tired, one should endeavour to avoid crudity, Maria.

Maria. Beast! (*Moves* R.)

Helen (L. *of* Duke). I'm afraid I didn't put quite enough milk in it, George dear.

Duke. I agree! But what it lacks in milk it makes up for in rice! (*Digs a fork into it.*)

Maria. Throw it at him!

Duke. I can quite see why you don't keep your servants, Maria.

Helen. George, please!

Duke. Have I said the wrong thing again?

Maria (*going back to him*). That is the second time you have suggested that it is through my fault my servants have left me.

Duke. I'll put it another way. I suggest one has to like you very much to remain in the same house with you, Maria darling.

Maria. Beast! (*She moves to him and pulls his nose.*) Beast!
(*Turning away to* R., *she goes out by the door below the porch.*)

(*The* Duke *holds his handkerchief to his face.*)

DUKE. It's too soon to tell, but I may have to ask you to fetch me a doctor, Helen.

HELEN (L. *of table*). Don't be ridiculous! Finish your lunch!

DUKE. To describe a kick in the face from a horse as ridiculous is to me a little unsympathetic. Why isn't the damned thing bleeding?

HELEN. I'm inclined to think it served you right. What pleasure do you derive from always irritating Maria as you do?

DUKE. I irritate her? I'm charming to her! Not once have I, for Richard's sake, told her she is a disagreeable old devil!

HELEN. She's not as bad as that.

DUKE. Why did her servants leave her?

HELEN. Because——

DUKE. Why do you hesitate? You told me yourself that if you were a servant girl you would rather starve than work for her.

HELEN (*looks at door*). I had no idea you would repeat it so loudly when I said it.

DUKE. Let her hear it, it would do her good!

HELEN. Please, George! With all her faults, I am *fond* of Maria.

DUKE (*angrily*). Do you think she's nice to Richard who adores her and waits on her hand and foot?

HELEN. I think she *means* to be.

DUKE. You know that isn't true—you said so yourself.

(HELEN *looks at door.*)

I want her to hear me, I tell you! She nags him, orders him about, won't let him do this or that—give me an answer! Have you ever in your life met with such selfishness?

HELEN. Yes! Once.

DUKE. You're lucky—I never have! It angers me so much I have difficulty in controlling myself!

HELEN (*crossing to* R.). George, dear, the more I see of you, the more I realize you're cursed with too great a sense of humour.

DUKE. How true that is! I believe that if Maria were to come into the room now—(*holds his face*)—and with a pain still acute—and she were to say that she was sorry, I honestly believe I'd forgive her! (*He pauses.*) I'm sure I should!

HELEN. I think that's wonderful!

(RICHARD *enters from the porch* R.; *he is carrying parcels.* HELEN *goes to him up* C.; *her manner is very sympathetic.*)

Richard, my poor sweet—twice up that dreadful hill! You must be exhausted! (*Takes parcels from him and puts them on table at back* R. *of the fireplace.*)

RICHARD. Thank you, Helen! I am rather! Where's Maria?

(*He fans himself with his hat and comes down* R. *at the back of the settee.*)

HELEN. In the kitchen!

RICHARD. Is she all right?

HELEN (*coming down a little* R.C.). Perfectly.

DUKE. That is not true. Richard, I have some bad news for you.

RICHARD (*anxiously*). Maria's annoyed with me for being so long? (*Comes to* R. *of table* L.C. *and sits on the arm of the chair* L. *of the fire.*)

DUKE. No! What do you think? She pulled my nose!

RICHARD. What for?

(HELEN *moves to the fireplace.*)

DUKE. I've no more idea than you have!

RICHARD. Ho! Well, it doesn't seem to have improved it!

DUKE. You—(*rising*)—I can't believe it! As she pulled my nose I said to myself, "If anything will infuriate Richard with her, this will!"

RICHARD. Well, it hasn't! And if she pulled your nose, she had some excellent reason for doing so. (*Takes out his pipe.*)

DUKE. And this is the return I get for coming up here to stand by you, remaining under the most extreme discomfort and insults to help you to win her——

RICHARD (*rising*). Let me tell you something. I haven't a chance in the world of winning her—but if I had, it would be in spite of you. At least fifty times you've nearly damned my chances! (*He seats himself in the chair.*)

DUKE (*indignantly*). I wish to leave you! Richard—give me my " Times."

RICHARD. I hadn't time to get it!

DUKE (*angrily*). You mean to tell me you haven't brought me my " Times " ?

RICHARD. I haven't!

DUKE. Well, of all the selfish devils that—— (*Throws down his table-napkin and sits at the table again.*)

(MARIA *enters* R.)

MARIA (*up* R.C.). So you're back? I suppose you forgot I told you I wanted these things at once? (*Looking at packages.*)

RICHARD (*rising*). I know I've been a long time, but there were so many things to buy that——

MARIA. It's all right. (*Moving down to the front of the settee.*) I expect you met a friend.

HELEN (*moving from the fire to the top of the settee*). Maria darling, you obviously have no idea what it *means* to climb that hill twice in one day.

C

Maria. Nonsense! Just what he wants! (*She sits on the lower arm of the settee.*) Does him all the good in the world!

Duke. Yes.

Maria (*to* Richard). Yes. Were you able to buy everything?

Richard. Everything. (*Sits again in the chair* l. *of the fireplace.*)

Duke (*rising*). That is not true—he did not bring me my "Times."

Maria. Sit down—

(*The* Duke *sits.*)

and try and alter your monotonous voice!

Richard. I agree! It drives one mad!

Duke. Don't pander to her, Richard, merely because you wish to make a good impression.

Richard. I am being perfectly natural! I agree with her!

Duke. Then why did you tell me the night before we left London that my voice was my chief asset?

Maria. Did you tell him that, Richard?

Richard. I may have done. I only know that unless you keep telling him he's something that he isn't, he sulks. The gramophone records are in the brown paper parcel, darling.

(Helen *goes up to the table* r. *of the fire and looks over the parcels.*)

Maria. Oh, that was nice of you to bring them—I'm so glad!

Duke. I hate gramophones.

Maria. You sent my telegram?

Richard (*rising with a start*). Ho!

Maria (*looking up, and leaving the arm of the settee*). Richard, you don't mean to tell me you forgot to send it?

(Helen *looks round.*)

Richard (*coming* c.). I'm terribly sorry, but I'm afraid I did.

Maria. This is too bad! Do you realize I won't have a single thing to read for two whole days?

Richard. I know, and I can't tell you how sorry I am!

(Helen *comes down to* Richard's r.)

Maria. What's the use of being sorry? If I'd known you were not going to send it, I should have gone myself. That's too annoying—— But I notice you've brought all the things you want! (*She goes back and rests on the lower arm of the settee.*)

(Helen *whispers to* Richard.)

Helen. Tell her to go to hell!

Richard (*starts*). What did you say?

HELEN (*as* MARIA *looks round at them, speaks ordinarily*).   I said you looked tired and not at all well.

RICHARD.   I'm all right, really I am——

MARIA.   Of course he's all right.

(HELEN *turns up to the fireplace.*)

RICHARD.   Maria, I would like you to believe me——

MARIA (*rising*).   Please don't worry—it was not important— (*she moves up at the back of the settee*)—it was only my books, and I realize it's too much to expect anyone to remember such a trivial thing.   I should have gone myself.

(*Exits through door* R. *below the porch.*)

DUKE.   If I walked up that hill twice and a woman spoke to me like that, I——

RICHARD (*moving down* R.).   Well, as you haven't walked up once, mind your own business.   She asked me particularly to telegraph for her books, and I realize it's most disappointing, and I'm terribly sorry.

DUKE.   You make me sick!   (*Looks at* RICHARD.)

RICHARD (*turns to him*).   I will make you sick if you're not careful, George.   (*He goes up at back of settee.*)

DUKE.   Helen, I would like you to walk with me.   I am anxious to read you my letter to the " Morning Post."

RICHARD.   If you have any decency you'll go and send that telegram for Maria.   (*He sits on the up-stage end of the settee.*)

DUKE.   *I?*   Walk up that hill (*pointing* R.) because Maria wants to read ?   Don't be funny !   There's a book in the house she should read.   Do you know what it is ?

(HELEN *gets a tray from the fireplace and goes behind the* DUKE *to the* L. *end of the table.*)

RICHARD.   No.

DUKE.   The Bible.

RICHARD.   What do you know about the Bible ?

DUKE.   More than you think I do.   It's full of examples to selfish women !

RICHARD.   Any for selfish men ?

DUKE.   Yes.   Read about Judas and you'll find he was the type of fellow who was too lazy to bring his friend " The Times."

(HELEN *loads tray at the table.*)

RICHARD.   Do you know you're very nearly an idiot !

DUKE.   Am I ?   (*He rises.*)   Will you walk, Helen ?

HELEN (*having packed up the lunch things on tray*).   If you mean it, George.

DUKE (*moving round the* R. *end of the table*).   I don't understand.

HELEN (*behind the table*). So often after I've taken the trouble
to change my clothes you've changed your *mind*.
DUKE. I mean to walk. (*He moves down* L.)
HELEN. Very well. (*She crosses with the tray behind the table to*
RICHARD.) I was right when I told you to—— (*Pauses.*) You
didn't look at all well, Richard.

(*She goes above the settee and exits* R. *with the tray.*)

(RICHARD *rises and follows* HELEN *to the door* R., *then smiles, bursts
into gentle laughter and moves down behind the settee.*)

DUKE. May I take part in the joke ?
RICHARD (*whose pipe is out, feels for matches*). No, you can't.
Ho ! I nearly forgot—I met the telegraph boy coming up the hill
and he gave me this telegram for you. (*He crosses to the* DUKE.)

(*The* DUKE *takes it from him, and puts it in his pocket unopened.*)

DUKE. Thank you.
RICHARD. Don't you open telegrams ?
DUKE. Not the ones I send myself.
RICHARD. What did you send yourself one for ?
DUKE. Tell me your joke and I'll tell you.
RICHARD. Very well. When Helen said " I don't think you
look at all well," I thought she said " Tell her to go to hell ! "
DUKE. I would have you know, Richard, my fiancée is not in
the habit of using that type of language.
RICHARD. Fiancée ? Are you and Helen going to be married ?
DUKE. We are.
RICHARD. I feel hurt. I think she should have told me.
DUKE. She couldn't—she doesn't know herself yet.
RICHARD. What do you mean ?
DUKE (*crossing to* R.). You might have thought I'd been wasting
my time here. I haven't, believe me. (*Turns round below the settee
to face* RICHARD *and works back to him.*) I have been studying Helen
very carefully ; and I have come to the profound conclusion,
Richard, that she is in every way a fit person to be the Duchess of
Bristol.
RICHARD. I agree. (*Sits on edge of table.*)
DUKE. She has the disadvantage of having no family behind
her, as it were. Her father, unfortunately, was only a pickle-maker
—but by nature she is a lady. And as I have to marry, Richard, I
prefer to marry Helen than anyone I know, even though at first I
realize my family will strongly disapprove. (*Takes out cigar-case.*)
RICHARD. Why should they ? Helen is one of the nicest women
in the world.
DUKE. I agree.

RICHARD (*moving to him*). I didn't know you had any cigars.
DUKE (*puts cigar-case quickly away*). I brought only fifty;
consequently I only smoked them when you were not here.
RICHARD. You mean devil! (*Returns—sits on table.*)
DUKE (L. *of* C.). Only where cigars are concerned. To continue:
(*lights cigar*) I have resolved, Richard, to play my part. In
addition to the position I give her, I am going to compel myself
to make her a good and faithful husband. (*Crosses to* R.)
RICHARD. Very kind of you.
DUKE (*moving back to* RICHARD). Let me tell you this: it's a
most unusual thing in our family.
RICHARD. I suppose there is no doubt she will marry you?
DUKE. Leaving me out of it, are you suggesting that any woman
would refuse to be the Duchess of Bristol?
RICHARD. No, that's true. (*Lights cigar.*)
DUKE. Don't be childish. There isn't a mother in London
with an eligible daughter who won't read the news with pain.
RICHARD. True! True!
DUKE (*crosses to* R.). The relief at having made up one's mind
is considerable. I can now return to London the same careless
fellow you've always known me. Hence this telegram. I am
urgently required in London, and I think I deserve a few days'
amusement. (*He sits on the settee.*)
RICHARD. Is Helen returning with you?
DUKE. Helen will return with you and Maria.
RICHARD (*moves to him*). If you wait until to-morrow, I might
be able to come with you.
DUKE. Why, are you going to leave the old——
RICHARD. George! Maria is expecting two more servants
to-morrow and if they come there will be nothing more that I can
do for her.
DUKE. You're through with her?
RICHARD. The reverse—she's through with me. (*He moves* L.)
DUKE. Has she told you so?
RICHARD. Every time she speaks to me. I've got on her nerves,
George—the poor dear simply can't bear me. It's a pity and I'm
sorry, but there it is.
DUKE. Don't be a fool! She's always like this.
RICHARD. George, I've known Maria all my life. I've never
known her like this. (*He goes to the top of the settee.*)
DUKE. Leave her and come with me to-night!
RICHARD. Certainly not! Nothing would induce me to leave
her as long as I can be of use to her.
DUKE. Noble, I call it! An idea! The moment I'm married,
you can make our house your home, Richard.
RICHARD. Thank you, George, that's charming of you. (*He
moves up to the fireplace.*)

DUKE. And I'll go further. My word, I'm a good friend! I'll insist on Helen making you a small allowance!

RICHARD. Certainly not!

DUKE. Very well! But don't you ever forget that I made you a damn good offer! (*He turns his back to* RICHARD *and stretches himself out on the settee.*)

RICHARD. An offer you should be ashamed of! (*He sits in the chair* R. *of the fireplace.*)

DUKE. Well, I'm not! I'm what an American friend of mine would describe as the far-seeing son of a gun! (*He settles himself with great comfort in settee.*) Nice cigar, Richard.

RICHARD (*settling himself apparently for sleep*). Very.

DUKE (*sinking further into the settee*). I shall live in the country a good deal when I'm married. It will keep one away from temptation.

RICHARL. I love the country!

DUKE. In my case I can see that marriage will have many advantages.

RICHARD. I can't begin to tell you how I envy you.

DUKE. And it's not as though one had not had a good time!

RICHARD. True.

DUKE (*closing his eyes*). I have very expensive but very pleasant memories of women, Richard.

RICHARD. I have only loved one woman all my life.

DUKE. Pity. You've missed a good deal. It's fun while it lasts.

RICHARD. Ive always believed that——

DUKE. You knew Molly?

RICHARD. Just.

DUKE. My word, she was expensive—but she was a sweet woman! Very sweet. I liked Molly. (*Pause.*) Very much.

(*They both are asleep.*)

(MARIA *enters from the door* R. *She first notices the* DUKE. *She looks at him from the back of the settee, then sees* RICHARD *and goes to his chair and is about to wake him—hesitates—and deliberately crosses to the gramophone* L. *and starts it.* RICHARD *waking with great suddenness, jumps up to* C.)

RICHARD. Damn it, is there no peace in this house?

DUKE (*sitting up*). I agree!

MARIA (L.). That is very, very interesting!

(DUKE *lies down again.*)

RICHARD (C.). I am sorry, Maria! You frightened me, I was asleep.

MARIA. Really?

RICHARD. You know how one says things when one is half unconscious.

MARIA. Perfectly. (*She moves to his* L.) The last person I was married to was frequently in that condition, and I found that was the only time he spoke the truth.

RICHARD. But you know I didn't mean it ?

MARIA. Then why say it ?

RICHARD (*irritably*). Good heavens, woman, surely——

MARIA. And don't call me " woman " and don't shout at me— I'm not deaf ! And if you must smoke cigars, which I've told you I hate, you might at all events try not to drop your ash on the floor ! Get something and clear it up.

RICHARD. Yes, darling. (*He turns to the fireplace and gets the hearth-broom and the coal-shovel and commences to sweep up the cigar-ash.*)

MARIA (*pointing*). There's another little bit there.

(*As* MARIA *directs him* RICHARD *obediently follows with the broom and shovel (ad. lib.). At the last he is stooping with his back to the settee and the* DUKE *lifts his foot to kick him, but* RICHARD *just saves himself looking indignant.* MARIA, *who has been moving about pointing out the ash, works to below the table and then gets over to the* L.)

Richard—I am sorry your afternoon sleep was disturbed by me— very sorry.

(*She exits* L.)

RICHARD (*replacing things at fireplace*). That, I think, has put the lid on it. What would you advise me to do ? (*Comes down* C.)

DUKE. I've made it a rule in my life not to be concerned in any inquest. She's a most unreasonable woman.

RICHARD. I've never known her like this. And she always gave me the impression before I came here that she liked me. It's a great pity. (*He moves to* L.)

(HELEN *enters* R., *she is dressed for walking. She comes above the settee to* C., *putting on her gloves.*)

HELEN. Anything the matter ?

RICHARD. There is rather. Being a little tired, I unfortunately fell asleep, and Maria woke me with great suddenness by playing the gramophone ; with the result I unhappily inquired if there was no damn peace in this house.

HELEN. Was she hurt or angry, Richard dear ?

RICHARD. Hurt, I think.

HELEN (*nodding her head*). I expect so.

RICHARD. I could kick myself. (*To her.*) What do you think the best thing to do ?

HELEN. George dear, I wonder if you would see if I left a letter on the table by the front door ?

DUKE. With pleasure. (*He rises, goes out to the porch and looks behind the open outer door, closing it to do so.*)

HELEN (*goes to* RICHARD). Tell her to go to hell! (*Spelling.*) " H-E-double L."

(*The* DUKE *returns.*)

DUKE (R.C.). There is no letter here.

HELEN. Off you go, Richard, you'll be *so* much happier when you've made your peace with Maria.

RICHARD. You don't understand, Helen. (*Crosses to* L.)

HELEN. Believe me, I do, Richard darling.

(RICHARD *exits* L.)

[*Looking after* RICHARD L.C.). There's one of the sweetest men I have ever known ; and although I have known him all my life it was not until this three weeks which I've spent with him here that I realized how nice he is.

DUKE (C.). I agree. I made him a devilish good offer just now, and he refused it. But I'm going to insist on his accepting it.

HELEN. I hope you will. (*Turning to the* DUKE.) Are you ready, George ?

DUKE (*looking up* L.C. *towards the window*). Look! The sun's gone.

HELEN (*endeavouring not to show her annoyance*). You mean you don't want to walk ?

DUKE. Of course I want to walk, but I'm thinking entirely of you—the sun has gone ! And incidentally, Helen, I've had some very bad news from London.

HELEN. I'm sorry ! It means that you will have to leave for London at once, I'm sure !

DUKE. I've thought out every conceivable way in which I might avoid it—but, alas ! There is no way ! I literally have to tear myself away to-night.

HELEN. I'm sorry. So we don't walk. (*Taking gloves off slowly and moving a little* L.)

DUKE. If you don't mind very much.

HELEN. Not at all. I understand.

DUKE. That's where you're so delightful, Helen, you *do* understand. (*He goes to her* R. *hand.*)

HELEN. I hope you will always think so, George dear.

DUKE. I shall, believe me. You don't mind cigars ?

HELEN. I like them.

DUKE. Helen, I am anxious to tell you something that has been in my mind for some considerable time.

HELEN. Please do.

DUKE. I beg of you not to consider it the impulse of youth, or the lack of much consideration.

HELEN. I won't, George dear.

DUKE. Very well. There is only one woman in the world that I would ask to be the Duchess of Bristol.

HELEN. That is very interesting, George.

DUKE. And if you will ask me who she is, I will tell you.

HELEN. Who is she, George ?

DUKE. You, Helen!

HELEN. I am very touched, and very flattered.

DUKE. And I'm very happy. (*Bends down and kisses her on the forehead. Moves away* R.)

HELEN. Thank you, George dear. (*Advancing to him a little.*) And I would like to tell you that I suppose in the whole world there is only one woman who'd refuse to be the Duchess of Bristol ; and if you will ask me who she is, I'll tell you.

DUKE. Er—er—who is she ?

HELEN. Me, George darling.

DUKE. Do I hear correctly that you refuse my offer of marriage ?

HELEN. Your hearing is perfect.

DUKE. You refuse ? You refuse—to be the Duchess of Bristol ?

HELEN. I do!

DUKE. May I ask why ?

HELEN. Only because *you* are the Duke, George.

DUKE. Only because—— (*He looks at her in astonishment.*) Are you insulting me, Helen ?

HELEN. Not nearly as much as you have insulted me.

DUKE. What do you mean ?

HELEN. You should have only asked me for my money. You should *not* have included *me* with it.

DUKE. Do you suggest that I asked you to be my wife merely on account of your money ?

HELEN. But didn't you ?

DUKE. I indignantly and emphatically say I did not.

HELEN. Then (*she turns away a little and looks down*) tell me the colour of my eyes.

(*The* DUKE *hesitates.*)

DUKE. Blue.

HELEN (*facing him*). Look.

DUKE (*looking*). Grey. (*He moves up stage uncomfortably.*)

HELEN. So *that* was easily settled. (*Crosses to the settee.*)

(*There is a pause.*)

I do hope it will not mean your having to send yourself another telegram, George. (*She sits on the settee.*)

DUKE (*coming down* c.). And I thought all this time that you liked me.

HELEN. Three weeks ago I adored you. If you'd asked me to marry you, run away with you without being married to you—if you'd asked me anything, I would have done it! I adored you so much!

DUKE. Then why won't you now?

HELEN. I have been alone with you three weeks.

DUKE. Well?

HELEN. And I realize you are charming, until one gets used to you, to look at—(*shakes her head*)—but nothing else. It's been my greatest disappointment.

DUKE. You are telling me that I died on you, is that it?

HELEN. The second day.

DUKE. Indeed. Well, that is not the experience of other women who have known me, believe me.

HELEN. May I be frank?

DUKE. I insist!

HELEN. Other women who have known you put up with your boredom, George, until they got the family jewels—and then they left you. But my case is rather different. I'm not only asked to return the family jewels, but I am asked to remain with the boredom!

DUKE. Refuse to marry me if you like, but don't be impertinent!

HELEN. You asked me to be frank!

DUKE. Boredom, indeed! It may interest you to know that I am always being asked to dinner-parties because I am amusing!

HELEN (*rising*). A dinner-party lasts two hours—(*as she crosses to* L.) marriage has been known to last for two years. But you are not in that danger, George.

DUKE. I'm sure you won't believe it, but there are many women who would be delighted to marry me.

HELEN. I'm sure there are many women who would like to be the Duchess of Bristol. Frankly, I rather wanted to be myself, until I spent three weeks with you.

DUKE. Really, how kind!

HELEN (*approaching him a little*). I know you hate being talked to like this, because you are unused to it. But your contribution to life, George darling, is that you allowed your mother to bring you into the world, and having done that, you were quite satisfied that everyone else who has been brought into it is for the purpose of approving of you!

DUKE. I'm not aware of it!

HELEN. Of course you're not. I should be angry with you if you were. But take it from one who once believed she loved you —your conceit is beyond imagination, your selfishness has no comparison. May I give you a word of advice?

DUKE. It depends——

HELEN (*looking off* L.). Marry Maria.

DUKE. How dare you! Are you being funny?

HELEN. Not at all! But for selfishness, you would both win the cup outright. She has money—you'd have a grand time!

DUKE. If a man had said that to me, I would have knocked him down. Do you mean to tell me that I'm anything like that old——

HELEN. Only your clothing distinguishes you.

DUKE. It's a filthy lie—I haven't one single thing in common with her. (*He moves to the settee and sits.*)

HELEN. Nonsense! If you don't get your own way about everything, you sulk. So does Maria. If Richard, who has walked up that hill twice, forgets your " Times " you are injured. If he doesn't wait on her hand and foot, she is angry. So are you!

DUKE. I've never allowed Richard to wait on me once.

HELEN. Only because you've been too busy allowing me to.

DUKE. But I thought you liked it?

HELEN (*going above him at the settee*). You thought I liked waiting on you as though I were a servant girl?

DUKE. You didn't say you didn't.

HELEN. George dear, there's one thing I like about you. You are the living illustration of the puerility of bringing a stupid man into the world with a title, and taking a useful man out of it without one.

DUKE (*after looking at her*). What an escape!

HELEN. Thank you, George!

DUKE. I was speaking for myself. Phew! I would have married you! Anyway, yours is a grand position—I envy you! It's something for a profiteer's daughter to have refused a duke!

HELEN (*controlling herself with difficulty*). I can be a cad-girl too! (*She moves to the table.*)

DUKE. I know it!

HELEN (*turning*). Many years ago there was a butcher's shop. An august person passing it one day was not attracted by the meat in the shop, but by the butcher's wife. The butcher with an ambitious eye to a knighthood, encouraged him to pass it frequently—with the result he became a baronet. The butcher's wife was encouraged—she acquired an ambition—so she left the butcher, with the result a son was born a duke. So far as I can see, the only difference between our families is—my father only profiteered in pickles.

(*There is a pause—*HELEN *takes a cigarette from the box on the table and lighting it looks at the* DUKE *and gives it to him. He takes it quite naturally, puts it in his mouth and smokes it. She laughs.*)

DUKE. What are you laughing at?

(HELEN *goes back to the table, takes another cigarette, and lights it.*)

HELEN. You're divine, George dear. I hope I shall always know you. (*She moves up to the fireplace.*)

(MARIA *enters* L.)

MARIA. Hasn't Richard brought tea yet?

HELEN. No. Poor darling, is he making tea?

MARIA (L.C.). I told him to bring it ages ago. I thought you were going for a walk.

HELEN. George and I decided that as the sun was gone, and as it was very comfortable here, we wouldn't.

MARIA (*looking at the* DUKE *who is gazing into space*). Is anything the matter with him?

HELEN. George has had some rather bad news, Maria.

MARIA. Is it bad enough?

HELEN. I think so.

MARIA. That's splendid! (*Moves up* L. *of table.*)

(RICHARD *enters* R., *carrying a tray of tea things. He passes above the top of the settee and places the tray on the table* L.C. *in front of* MARIA.)

RICHARD. Here we are. A little tea, a little cake, a little toast —and who cooked it, I ask?

MARIA (*sitting at the back of the table and commencing to pour the tea*). And who forgot to send my telegram, may *I* ask?

RICHARD (R. *of her*). All right, I'll go down after tea and send it.

(HELEN *moves down and sits on the upper arm of the settee.*)

MARIA. And look sad all the evening. No, thank you, Richard.

RICHARD. If you had had the telephone put in, you could send for a million books a day.

MARIA. I'm not in the happy position of being able to spend pounds for a telephone which one would only use for a few months in the year—

(RICHARD *takes tea to* HELEN.)

but perhaps you are.

HELEN (*to* RICHARD). You don't look at all—(*spelling*) W-E-double L.

RICHARD (*who has handed* HELEN *the cup and moved, turns quickly to her*). Certainly not!

MARIA. Will you stop that whispering!

(RICHARD *goes to the* R. *of the table, takes his own tea and goes up* C.)

HELEN (*getting off the arm of the settee, sits beside the* DUKE *on his* L. *hand and touches him*). Do you begin to see the likeness, George?

(*All through the preceding scene the* DUKE *has been sitting in deep thought. Every time* MARIA *speaks it appears to jar on him. He now jumps up and starts to walk out by the porch.*)

HELEN. Where are you going, George ?

DUKE (*up* R.C.). I'm going to the village.

MARIA. What for ?

DUKE. To send the telegram that Richard forgot to send for you.

MARIA (*dropping the teapot*). Help !

RICHARD (*spills some tea over his clothes*). Look what you've done, you fool !

HELEN. Have your tea first, George.

(MARIA *pours it out.*)

DUKE. Very well. (*He crosses to the table.*)

(MARIA *watches him and passes him the cup.*)

Thank you very much, Maria, you are very kind !

(MARIA *starts, looks at him, then at the others.*)

HELEN. Any sugar there, Richard ?

RICHARD. Sugar ? Sorry, I forgot it. (*Starts to go for it.*)

DUKE (*stopping him gently*). You are tired. (*Crossing* RICHARD *to door* R.) I will get it ! (*He goes out by the door* R. *below the porch.*)

(RICHARD *up* R.C. *looks after him.*)

MARIA. All this before he sets fire to the house ?

HELEN (*laughs*). I don't think so.

RICHARD. But something is wrong with him ! I believe he's dangerous.

(*The* DUKE *re-enters and passing in front of* RICHARD, *to the settee, hands the sugar to* HELEN.)

DUKE. Sorry I've been so long.

(*They all look at one another.* MARIA *rises.*)

RICHARD (C.). Don't you feel well, dear old George ?

DUKE. I feel terribly well, thank you. (*He moves across to the table* L.C. *and places the sugar basin on it at the same moment* MARIA *edges towards* RICHARD.)

MARIA (*whispering to* RICHARD). He can't be. You know his grandmother was a little touched.

(*The* DUKE *walks to the gramophone* L. *and starts it, and then sits on the stool in front of it.*)

DUKE. Pretty, don't you think ?

MARIA (*clutching* RICHARD'S *arm*). Take it off, Richard, I'm suffocating!

DUKE. Sorry, Maria dear. I put it on for you. I thought you liked it. (*He gets up and stops the gramophone.*)

RICHARD (*crossing to the* DUKE). George, I've had enough of this!

DUKE. Enough of what?

RICHARD. This fooling. Can't you see that you're frightening Maria?

DUKE. I'm very sorry, Maria dear, I didn't mean to. I'm very sorry. (*Takes off his coat.*)

MARIA. Look! (*Shrinking back to up* R.C.)

RICHARD (*to him*). Careful, George old man, careful!

DUKE (*advancing to the door* R., *rolling up his sleeves*). It's my turn to do the washing up! Don't hurry with your tea. I'm only going to put the kettle on.

(*He walks up past* MARIA, *who steps back towards the fireplace as he moves to the door* R. *and goes out.*)

(MARIA *walks on tiptoe to the door* R. *and looks out.*)

RICHARD (*in front of the table* L.C.). What's he doing?

(*Crash off.*)

MARIA. Ho! He's kicked the coal-scuttle over. (*Starts.*) He's struck a match!

(RICHARD *advances to up* R. *of* C.)

No, no, it's all right, he's lit a cigarette. (*Moving at top of the settee to* RICHARD *and, as she speaks, crossing him to down* L.C.) Richard, I'm going to my room. Fetch the doctor and ask him to take him away. And if George asks where I am, tell him I've gone for a long walk.

RICHARD. A long walk?

MARIA. A very long walk.

(MARIA *goes out* L.)

RICHARD (*up* C.). What's the matter with him?

HELEN (*rising and crossing to the table, putting down her cup*). Nothing at all. I put him on my knee and smacked him hard for the first time in his life. That's all.

(*The* DUKE *re-enters from the door* R.)

Shall I see you before you go, George dear?

DUKE (*coming above the settee to down* R.C., *putting on his jacket*). No.

HELEN. Very well! Good-bye and a pleasant journey! And

if ever another girl falls in love with you, *marry* her the NEXT DAY. (*Moves* L.) It's your only chance, my sweet. (*She exits* L.)

DUKE (*sitting on the settee*). Did you hear that?

RICHARD (C.). Yes.

DUKE. She's been hurling those things at me in dozens!

RICHARD (*coming towards the* DUKE). I don't understand a damn thing you're talking about. Why are you behaving like an idiot, frightening Maria and all of us?

DUKE. I'm showing her, if I choose to be, I'm not a bit like Maria. Heavens! that hurt me badly!

RICHARD. What are you talking about?

DUKE. Now don't tell me I'm a liar, because I'm not! But what do you think she said to me when I asked her to marry me?

RICHARD. What?

DUKE. She told me that I'm an ass, I'm conceited, I'm selfish, I nag—I'm the descendant of a prostitute——

RICHARD. No, no!

DUKE (*angrily*). I tell you I am!—or she says I am. I'm a bore. And I'm everything that's rotten!

RICHARD. Well, well, I am amazed!

DUKE. What about me? What do you think I am? I've never been so disappointed in anybody in all my life. You know it's your old woman who's done this.

RICHARD. What old woman are you referring to?

DUKE. Yours.

RICHARD (R.C.). Maria is exactly one year younger than I am.

DUKE. How old are you?

RICHARD. Forty.

DUKE. She's a liar! She's forty-one. Born on the same day as my stepmother.

RICHARD. I believe Maria. Anyhow, how is she the cause of it?

DUKE. This taking you away for three weeks and our coming with you.

RICHARD. Explain.

DUKE. Helen's found out thousands of things about me she didn't know—and she doesn't like a single one of them.

RICHARD. Did you love her, George?

DUKE. How can a man, harassed to death with financial troubles like I am, be able to concentrate on love? It's unreasonable, Richard. Anyway, you go and get your old woman to turn you down and see how you like it!

RICHARD. Thank you, but I have more sense than you have. I'm not risking it. The moment the servants arrive to-morrow I leave a note telling her I am sorry but I've gone.

DUKE. Coward!

RICHARD. Not at all. I wish to spare her the embarrassment

of telling me that I've failed her. What are you going to do, George ?

DUKE. Something desperate.

RICHARD. George, we must make money.

DUKE. Try and forget I am a duke and talk sense.

RICHARD. How did you lose your money ?

DUKE. Women.

RICHARD. I mean how did you lose your big money ?

DUKE. Women.

RICHARD. Well, I didn't. I lost mine——

DUKE. Look out !

(MARIA *enters from recess* L. RICHARD *goes up* C.)

MARIA (*walking over to the* DUKE *and looking at him*). Are you better ?

DUKE (*still seated on the settee*). I was never ill.

MARIA. Well, I wish to tell you your behaviour was perfectly disgraceful !

DUKE (*rising*). And shall I tell you why my behaviour was perfectly disgraceful ?

MARIA (C.). I should like to know.

DUKE (R.C.). Well, I wished it to be known that I had not one single thing in common, nor am I in the least like——

RICHARD (*who has come down on* MARIA'S L.—*stops him*). George !

DUKE. Very well, for your sake I won't. (*He turns up stage* R.C.) But I am writing to you, Maria. (*He goes out by the door leading to the kitchen* R.)

MARIA (*following to up* R.C. *and looking after the* DUKE). It would please me very much if you gave that young man up as a friend.

RICHARD (C.). Oh, he's not a bad fellow—a little——

MARIA. I would like to think that you'd given him up.

RICHARD. I see your point.

MARIA. I've had a telegram. Those servants are unable to come. (*Moves to the front of the settee.*)

RICHARD. Why ?

MARIA. They've sent me an extremely rude telegram refusing. (*She sits on the settee.*)

RICHARD. Brutes ! No matter, if you will allow me, I'll continue to do my best while you are here.

MARIA. Thank you, Richard. That's very kind of you. Although we've only been here three weeks, I want to tell you something.

RICHARD (C.). It's all right, Maria, I know.

MARIA. How do you know ? Would you kindly be silent while I speak ? What I have to say is a little embarrassing, and you might realize it.

RICHARD. I know, and I'm sorry !

MARIA. I brought you here for the purpose of finding out, as you know, that if we married would there be a chance of us both being happy.

RICHARD. Quite. And I would like to say now——

MARIA. Would you please be quiet?

RICHARD. Sorry!

MARIA. When I left London, I liked you very much. I almost believed that you possessed qualities that would endear yourself to me.

RICHARD. I know. (*Shakes his head sorrowfully.*)

MARIA. But I had no idea, Richard, how nice you really are.

RICHARD (*amazed*). What did you say?

MARIA. What I was going to say, when you interrupted me, was that you are a thousand times nicer than I thought you were. And I'm——

RICHARD. One minute—I——

MARIA. Would you mind waiting one minute whilst I finish what I was going to say?

RICHARD. Go on!

MARIA. I'm not only going to marry you, but——

RICHARD (*starting*). What?

MARIA. Oh, don't keep interrupting. You're irritating me very much—— But to prove to you how much I trust you, I'm going to settle five thousand pounds a year on you for life. Are you pleased?

RICHARD. Pleased? But I am delighted!

MARIA. Ah!

RICHARD. And all this time I thought I'd been irritating you to death. I almost believed you disliked me. You'll never have any idea how miserable I've been.

MARIA. But why?

RICHARD. You were so intolerant—so horrid to me!

MARIA. Horrid to you? What are you talking about? I've never been so nice to anyone in my life before!

RICHARD. One minute. (*He moves a little nearer to her*). Let us straighten this out. You know you've tried every way of provoking me to see whether I was bad tempered or not.

MARIA. I did nothing of the kind. I wouldn't descend to anything so mean!

RICHARD. Nonsense, you know you did! You know you used to nag the life out of me to see if I would answer back—and a thousand other things you did.

MARIA. What are you talking about?

RICHARD (*with a start backwards to the upper end of the settee— and speaking incredulously*). Maria, you don't mean to tell me *that* has been really *you* all the time?

MARIA. Of course! Are you mad, Richard?

D

RICHARD. Is this how you would be if we married ?

MARIA. Of course !

RICHARD. Heaven be praised ! (*He puts his hand to his head and turns a little to his* L.)

MARIA. What for ?

RICHARD. That you took me away for three weeks on approval !

MARIA. Tell me what you mean ?

RICHARD. How much did you say you would settle on me ?

MARIA. Five thousand a year.

RICHARD. My income is three hundred a year—and I know what it's like to feel a millionaire ! (*Moves farther* L.)

MARIA (*rises*). Richard, are you insulting me ?

RICHARD. How long did your late husband live with you, Maria ?

MARIA. Eighteen years.

RICHARD. What a man ! What a constitution ! (*Moves still farther* L.)

MARIA (*moving to* C.). How dare you speak to me like that ?

RICHARD (*going to her*). If you had the slightest idea how you've spoken to me during the last three weeks, you would be sympathetic ! Maria dear, double that five thousand, treble that five thousand, give me every shilling you've got in the world, and *then* the answer would be " *No !* "

MARIA. I—I—have never been so degraded in all my life ! (*Goes down* R. *a little.*)

RICHARD (*following her to* R. *of* C.). When I left London with you, I thought as I have thought of you all my life—the nicest woman in the world ; the only woman I have ever liked. But obviously I never knew you at all. And these three weeks have made me realize that you are not and never have been one of the things I thought you.

(MARIA *sits again on the settee.*)

And as long as I live I will love you for having given me the opportunity of finding you out. I would have married you not knowing.

MARIA. You—you beast ! Go away !

RICHARD (*drawing himself up to his full height*). Before I go, Maria, I have only one other thing to say to you—may God bless you for your kindness and thoughtfulness to me. (*He turns up stage and goes out by the door* R. *below the porch.*)

(MARIA *weeps and screams.*)

(HELEN *enters from* L. *and comes over to* MARIA.)

HELEN. Darling, what is the matter ?

MARIA. He—he—he——

HELEN. Calm yourself, darling ! What is it ? (*She sits above* MARIA *on the settee and puts her arm round her.*)

MARIA. He has made me cry and——

(HELEN *pats her and comforts her.*)

HELEN. The brute ! And for the first time in your life, darling !
(*She looks towards the kitchen door and smiles.*)

MARIA (*rising and moving to* L.). I'm going to my room. I
couldn't bear the beast to come in here and find he had been able
to make me cry. (*She exits* L.)

(*Through the window snow can be seen falling.*)

(HELEN *rises and moves to* L.C.)

HELEN (*calling*). Richard !

(RICHARD *appears at the door* R.)

RICHARD. Has she gone ?

HELEN. Yes.

RICHARD (*coming into the room a little*). You're sure ?

HELEN. Yes. Where is George ?

RICHARD (*up* R.C.). Sitting in front of the kitchen fire, stunned
by the shock you gave him.

HELEN (L. *of table*). Maria's lying on her bed in the same condition. If anyone had told you and me three weeks ago that——

RICHARD. I wouldn't have believed them.

HELEN. Surely there must be deep down something rather nice
about George for me to ever have been able to like him as much
as I did. (*Moves to the chair at the back of the table and sits.*)

RICHARD. I suppose there must be about Maria. (*He sits on
the arm of the chair* R. *of the fireplace.*)

HELEN. Spoilt from the day of his birth—to make him a decent
man he needs six months before the mast as a common sailor——

RICHARD. Alone with Maria.

HELEN. He needs to suffer the degradation and the humiliations
of poverty——

(*The snow falls heavier.*)

RICHARD. Alone with Maria.

HELEN. Is there no way, Richard, we could do that for them ?

(RICHARD *shakes his head.*)

RICHARD. There must be.

HELEN. Let's think !

CURTAIN.

ACT III

SCENE.—*The same as Act II.*

TIME.—*Three hours later. A small chair from above the desk* R. *is placed at the* R. *end of the table* L.C.

(*The stage is empty.*)

(HELEN *enters* L. *carrying a travelling-bag, she hurries with it to the door of the porch. Puts the bag outside and closes the door again quickly. She then comes and sits* R. *end of table* L.C. MARIA *enters* L. *She walks quietly to the settee and sits down, gazing into space. Picks up a cushion and throws it across the room.*)

HELEN. Darling, you're losing control of yourself again!

MARIA. I—I—could scream the house down!

HELEN. Why don't you? It might do you good.

MARIA. How dare he stay here to-night!

HELEN. You must be reasonable. There's no train until six in the morning. Surely you don't expect him to wait on a cold railway platform all night, do you?

MARIA. Yes, I do!

HELEN. Nonsense! Besides, it is not as though they were annoying you by being in the same room; (*she rises, going* R.) they are sitting quietly together in the kitchen. (*At the door to the kitchen.*) Listen! Not a sound! You wouldn't know they were even in the house. And Richard will be gone by five. (*She comes to* R.C. *slightly above* MARIA.)

MARIA. Ho! To think that I brought the brute here to find out if I like him, and he has the audacity the moment I tell him I do, to tell me he doesn't like me!

HELEN. Outrageous! But wasn't that the idea?

MARIA. What do you mean? I didn't bring him here to find out if he liked me!

HELEN. No! How silly of me!

MARIA. Anyway, I don't know which of us is the luckier; I to have lost the vulgar man, or you to have discovered in time that you were anxious to marry a congenital idiot!

HELEN. George isn't entirely an idiot!

MARIA. Yes he is. Look at his face—" idiot " is written in block letters all over it.

HELEN (*shakes her head*). All I will admit is his face betrays a lack of something which is not unusual amongst members of very old families.

MARIA. Stop being a lady and say " idiot." Horrid man from the day of his birth.

HELEN (*sitting again in the chair* R. *end of table* L.C.). A month from to-day you won't recognize him, darling !

MARIA. That is my intention.

HELEN. I meant, he will be so different. Can you imagine George kindly, tolerant and unselfish—— ?

MARIA. Oh, don't talk such rubbish !

HELEN. He's going to be !

(DUKE *enters from the door to the kitchen* R. *He is wearing an overcoat.*)

MARIA. Who asked you to come in here ?

DUKE (R.C.). No one. But I have the alternative of either sitting with two extremely unpleasant women in here, or one strong, silent man in there. (*Crosses and sits on stool* L.)

HELEN. Have you quarrelled with Richard ?

DUKE. Ever since he ticked Maria off he is so conceited there's no holding him !

MARIA. Is he boasting that he " ticked me off," as you call it ?

DUKE. Naturally.

MARIA. May I ask what sort of things he has been saying about me ?

DUKE. He says he is going to make it his life's work from now on to make you a decent woman. And he says he has discovered the way to do it !

MARIA. How dare he say such a thing !

DUKE. I know ! I told him not to be a conceited ass—but he says it can be done ! He's very childish to-night.

HELEN. It sounds as though there were hope for you, George.

DUKE. If you have anything to say to me, would you kindly address me through a third person !

HELEN. Why are you wearing an overcoat, George dear ?

DUKE. That is entirely my business. But if you must know, that kitchen is one mass of blasted draughts.

MARIA. I am sure you would find the station platform much less uncomfortable than my house !

DUKE. Richard and I talked it over, and we decided we would find it exactly the same.

MARIA. Let me tell you one thing. If ever I meet you again after you leave here at five o'clock to-morrow morning, and you even dare to speak to me, I'll cut you publicly.

DUKE. If I ever speak to you again, Maria, I hope everyone will cut me publicly!

(HELEN *laughs*.)

MARIA. Oh, Helen, how can you laugh at that horrid man!

HELEN. I'm not laughing, darling. I was shocked by his impertinence!

DUKE (*rising and crossing to* MARIA). Mrs. Wislack, may I have the key of the alcohol cupboard?

MARIA. No, you may not!

DUKE. Very well, I won't, but may Heaven have mercy on you!

MARIA. Will you leave this room at once?

DUKE. I will not. I am suffering from rigour and I propose to continue with it in here! (*Moves up a little* C.)

(RICHARD *enters* R. *He is wearing an overcoat, the collar is turned up. He is also wearing gloves. He is in a temper.*)

RICHARD (*to* DUKE). You villain!

HELEN. What has he done?

RICHARD (R.C.). He stood by the other side of the door—I thinking he had found a place to avoid some of the draughts—when I discovered he was merely there to listen to your conversation in here!

MARIA. Ho! Is that true?

DUKE (C.). Absolutely!

RICHARD. And I am not dull!

MARIA. Yes, you are!

RICHARD. And I am not a vulgar little man!

MARIA. Yes, you are!

DUKE (*moving to down* L. *of* C.). You look vulgar, you are vulgar, and you're dull! I wish to make a pronouncement. My rigour is on the increase!

RICHARD. Did you have that whisky and soda as I told you?

DUKE. No! She whom you once loved refuses to cough up the key.

RICHARD. She refused! (*To* MARIA.) Give me the key of that cupboard which should never be locked. (*He points towards the door* R.)

MARIA. I will do nothing of the sort!

RICHARD. Give it to me, I tell you!

MARIA. I will not!

RICHARD. Then you put me in the hideous position of having to reveal myself as a man who has always known where it was!

(RICHARD *crosses above the* DUKE *to the cabinet* L., *puts his hand inside, finds the key and returns to* MARIA.)

MARIA. You—you—have had the audacity to go to that cupboard unknown to me ?

RICHARD (R.C.). Every night since I've been here I've covered my face—with the exception of that part which is used for the purpose of drinking—with shame !

MARIA. You—you——

DUKE. Do you mean to tell me that you had a whisky and soda every night without telling me about it ? (*He moves* L. *and again sits on the stool.*)

RICHARD. You had your cigar. And only because you're cold will I give you one now. Helen, be good enough to fetch him a small whisky and soda.

MARIA. She will do nothing of the sort.

RICHARD. Silence ! (*He moves to the door* R., *opens it and speaks to* HELEN *in a determined voice.*) Helen !

(HELEN *walks to the door ; as she passes through he whispers.*)

It's all right. I've put your bag in the car.

(HELEN *exits, taking the key from* RICHARD *as she does so.*)

(RICHARD *returns to* C.)

DUKE. How dare you whisper to my late fiancée ?

RICHARD (*sentimentally*). Ha ! (*Blows a kiss to the door* R.)

MARIA. Stop blowing kisses to a girl young enough to be your daughter !

RICHARD. Mrs. Wislack ! For me to be Helen's father, I should have had to be an enterprising boy of fifteen.

MARIA. Be quiet ! You're having the same effect on me as a small boat in a very rough sea.

DUKE (*rising*). Me too. (*He crosses to door* R.)

RICHARD. Where are you going ?

DUKE. I wish to speak to Helen.

RICHARD. Are you going to speak to Helen—or are you going to make that small whisky I ordered for you a large one ?

DUKE. How dare you, you cad !

(*The* DUKE *exits* R.)

MARIA. Oh ! I could cry with shame !

RICHARD (*smiling and moving a little nearer to her*). Which is precisely what you are going to do, lovey !

MARIA. Don't call me " lovey," you hateful creature !

RICHARD. But you are ! Maria, during the last five hours I have been thinking deeply, and I have come to two conclusions about myself !

MARIA. I have come to one without thinking !

RICHARD. First, I realize you love me very much !

(*She looks at him.*)

Second, you are right to !

MARIA. The moment you came into the room I thought I recognized the smell of cooking sherry !

RICHARD. And let me point this out to you, had it not been for my constant fidelity to you during the last fifteen years, I might be standing here to-night described by the world as the Napoleon of lovers !

MARIA. On the other hand, it's possible you might not !

RICHARD. True ! But I have no regrets ; and further, I still propose to remain faithful to the happy memories I have of you before I found you out !

MARIA. Thank you very much !

RICHARD. My epitaph will be, " He turned a woman who in her youth was one of the most unpleasant of God's creatures, into, in her middle age, a perfect pet ! " (*He moves a little to* L.)

MARIA. Indeed ! May I ask what I will be doing whilst you are attempting to do that ?

RICHARD (*smiling and turning*). Nothing ! You won't know until it's too late !

MARIA. Perhaps you would tell me what all this means ?

RICHARD (*returning and standing above her—bending over her*). It means that I have not finally, as it were, given you up !

MARIA. Talk stupidities if you must, but don't breathe over me —I hate it !

RICHARD. Try as I will, I still care for you, Maria.

MARIA. Don't waste any more of your time.

RICHARD. Nonsense ! One word from me, and you know you'd fall violently into my arms !

MARIA. If you don't leave me I certainly shall—but not in the sense you mean it.

RICHARD. Do you realize, Maria, you are still a very beautiful woman ?

MARIA. I do. And mind your own business !

RICHARD. It is my business. In a month from to-day, you will not only be beautiful, but you will be one of the sweetest women in the world.

MARIA. Please don't think me impertinent, but assuming it is necessary, how do you propose to do that ?

RICHARD. I expect so much from my idea that I even anticipate you will be so nice I shall find myself wanting to marry you all over again !

MARIA. Will you at once tell me what this is that you are threatening to do ?

RICHARD (*he takes a letter out of his pocket*). The facts are in this letter, which it is my intention to place on that table before I leave for London.

MARIA. Give it to me at once ! (*She tries to take it.*)

RICHARD (*holding it away from her*). Certainly not!

MARIA. Just as you like. Anyway, I don't suppose I shall ever read it!

RICHARD. You will read it again and again. And I have no hesitation in saying if the instructions are carried out it will make you the woman I thought you were three weeks ago. It may even mean that it will bring us such happiness that rather than ever be separated from each other again we—we——

MARIA. Will be the first married couple to swim the Channel!

RICHARD. Exactly!

(*She tries to snatch the letter from him.*)

Ha! (*He holds it away.*)

MARIA. Beast!

RICHARD. Your interest is awakened. That is all to the good!

MARIA. Go away—I'm going to cry!

RICHARD. You need not yet. That is part of the instructions in this letter. (*He turns to the front of the table, putting the letter in his pocket.*)

MARIA. You bully!

RICHARD (*turning to her*). The reverse. The most tender-hearted fellow in the world!

(*The* DUKE *enters* R. *He is smiling; he is not in any sense drunk.* RICHARD *moves towards him.*)

May I ask what's the matter with you?

DUKE (R.C.). There wasn't any soda.

MARIA. Look at it, I ask you!

DUKE. Look well—you see it for the last time.

RICHARD. I'm ashamed of you!

DUKE. That's disappointing, because I am delighted with myself. (*To* MARIA.) You naughty old lady, locking up such beautiful whisky!

MARIA. Go to bed, you disgusting creature! What can you do with it?

RICHARD. Nothing—it has never been able to do anything with itself.

DUKE. He who insults me takes from me nothing. He who takes from me my honour, taketh all. Shakespeare.

RICHARD. I bet you five pounds you don't even know who Shakespeare was.

DUKE. He was the fellow with a place at Stratford.

RICHARD. Give me that key!

(*The* DUKE *gives it him.*)

Why did you give it me without a protest?

DUKE (*smiles*). I have my reasons.

RICHARD. You—you've drunk it all ? If you have, George, you will pay for it and pay very dearly.

DUKE. I fear nothing—that's the type of fellow I am!

RICHARD (*crossing in front of the* DUKE *above the settee towards door* R.). Very well——

MARIA. You're not leaving me with this horrid little person, are you ?

RICHARD. For the moment. I am going to see if my suspicions are correct. (*Exits* R.)

DUKE (*moving down* L.C.). Boasting brute!

(MARIA *rises and walks round the lower end of the settee towards the door to the kitchen.*)

(*Moving up* R.C.) Mrs. Wislack, I don't wish to speak to you, but I have to!

MARIA (R. *up stage*). I'm very sorry, but I don't wish to speak to you.

DUKE (*turning to the chair* R. *of table* L.C. *and moving it slightly*). Will you kindly be seated—I feel less frightened of you when you are sitting down. (*He moves down* L.)

MARIA (*coming to the chair* R. *of table*). Say what you have to say and say it quickly! (*She sits in the proffered chair.*)

DUKE. Very well. (*He crosses in front and sits on the settee.*) In the cause of both our futures, are you prepared to call a truce for the space of five minutes only of our dislike of each other ?

MARIA. The reason ?

DUKE. Love.

MARIA. Five minutes.

DUKE. In a few hours from now, Richard and myself will have left this house for ever.

MARIA. Thank Heaven!

DUKE. That isn't true. And moreover, if he goes to-morrow morning, you may lose him entirely—he may never want to see you again !

MARIA. I hope he won't!

DUKE. Very well. (*He rises and moves away round the lower end of the settee to door* R.)

MARIA. Come here. What were you going to say ?

DUKE (*moving above the settee towards her*). Are you going to stop pretending ?

MARIA. Yes.

DUKE (C.). Do you like him or not ?

MARIA. Yes.

DUKE (*going nearer to her*). Do you want him to catch that six-o'clock train to-morrow morning ?

MARIA. No.

DUKE. Do you love him ?

MARIA. Don't shout!

DUKE (*louder*). Do you love him ?

MARIA. Yes—you beast ᵢ

DUKE. Then why don't you say so ?

MARIA. I suppose a woman's entitled to some modesty ?

DUKE. Not when you're on the verge of losing your loved one.

MARIA. You look ridiculous enough without looking sentimental. Having discovered all this, what does it mean ?

DUKE. I don't want to leave here at five o'clock to-morrow morning.

MARIA. Why not ?

DUKE (*moving towards the settee*). Because during the last few hours I too have discovered that I am in love.

MARIA. With yourself.

DUKE. If it comes to that—— (*He goes up behind her to the back of the table and takes a white handkerchief out of his pocket and puts it on the table between them.*)

MARIA. What is that for ?

DUKE. To remind us both there is a truce going on.

MARIA. Continue.

DUKE (*moving to the L. end of the table*). I have discovered that I am on the verge of losing one of the world's most exquisite people. Forgive me—I close my eyes. I see her divine face, her little hands, her unusual figure—her——

MARIA. Shut up !

DUKE (*points to handkerchief*). Oi !

MARIA. I beg your pardon !

DUKE. Granted. And as you don't understand romance, I'll put it briefly, I love her !

MARIA. What are you going to do about it ?

DUKE. I'm going to stay here. And you don't deserve it !—keep Richard here, too.

MARIA. How do you propose to do that ?

DUKE (*advancing to her at the back of the table*). In moments of seriousness such as this, damnable as it is, we must temporarily forget the word honour !

MARIA. That'll be easy for you !

(*The* DUKE *snatches up the handkerchief.*)

I beg your pardon !

(*He puts the handkerchief down again.*)

DUKE. Granted !

MARIA. What is your idea ?

DUKE (*sitting in the chair at the back of the table*). We must in some way invent a means whereby we will all stay here a little longer, thereby gaining time to win them back again !

MARIA. How do you propose to do all this ?

DUKE. Ah, that's the catch ! You can't think of any way, can you, without loss of dignity on either of our parts ?

MARIA. No, I can't !

(Pause.)

DUKE. How is your appendix ?

MARIA. Out.

DUKE. Yes—it would be. *(Eagerly.)* I have it !

MARIA. Tell me then.

DUKE. Look at me.

(She looks at him.)

How do I look ?

MARIA. Revolting !

DUKE. I mean in health.

MARIA. Anæmic.

DUKE. You don't look so damned——

(She points to handkerchief.)

I beg your pardon !

MARIA. Granted ! What are you intending to do ?

DUKE. I am proposing to suffer from some obscure disease which will make it impossible for you to send me out of the house in the morning.

MARIA. Go on !

DUKE. Moreover, it will be a disease which can only be nursed by a man. That's how I remain and also keep Richard.

MARIA. Do you think you can be convincing ?

DUKE *(rising and moving to* L. *of the table).* Having mentioned the words " obscure disease," I am not at all sure I haven't got one ! I suddenly feel very strange. I do hope I'm not going to be really ill. Anyway, this is not a time for cowardice.

MARIA. How do you propose to begin this ?

DUKE. I shall go at once to bed.

MARIA. Then—— ?

DUKE. Having given me time to fling myself upon my bed in a becoming attitude worthy of a sick man, you will call violently for Richard.

MARIA. Then—— ?

DUKE. You will describe my sudden collapse—how I clutched at my heart and screamed with pain. That's funny ! Having mentioned the word " heart " I have a pain !

MARIA. Wind.

DUKE. I am a gentleman, Mrs. Wislack.

MARIA. I beg your pardon ! Go on !

DUKE. And you realizing the seriousness of my condition ordered me to bed. Send Richard to me and I will do the rest.

MARIA. You think you will be able to convince him of your serious condition ?

DUKE. As easily as one could a doctor.

MARIA. How do you propose to do it ?

DUKE. I shall rely on simple groans. (*He picks up the handkerchief.*)

MARIA. I see. If we are going to do it, hadn't you better go ?

DUKE. You're right. (*Walks away to the entrance* L. *and returns.*) Having forgotten my hot-water bottle, wouldn't it be more convincing if you lend me yours ?

MARIA. I'm not surprised.

DUKE. If we had such a thing as a little Benger's Food in the house, a little brought to me in bed would not be unconvincing.

MARIA. What about a band from London ?

DUKE. And to ensure our success, you may find yourself having to wait on me a good deal.

MARIA. I knew from the beginning you'd get the best of this.

DUKE (*moving down* L.). Mrs. Wislack, be good enough to send Richard to me at once and remember I have undertaken the intelligent part. (*He exits* L.)

(MARIA *rises and appears to be thinking. She takes her handkerchief out and then calls.*)

MARIA. Richard ! Richard !

(HELEN *enters door* R.)

HELEN (*crossing to her*). Darling, what's the matter ?

MARIA (*wiping her eyes*). George.

HELEN. He's been rude to you ?

MARIA. No, no. I'm wondering if he'll ever be rude to anyone again.

HELEN. What do you mean ?

(RICHARD *enters* R.)

MARIA. Poor darling, we were sitting here talking to each other when suddenly he clutched at his heart, screamed with pain and collapsed violently on to the floor.

RICHARD (R.C.). Good heavens !

HELEN (C.). Where is he now ?

MARIA (L.C.). I don't know ! He recovered a little and said " I'm going to my bed. Send my dear old friend Richard to me." I was so stunned by the shock I was unable to help him.

RICHARD. Poor old fellow, I'll go to him at once.

(RICHARD *quickly crosses in front and exits* L.)

HELEN (*anxiously*). Is he terribly ill, do you think ?

MARIA. Terribly. Nice little man, so courageous—I feel so upset !

HELEN. I shall go to him! (*Moves as if going* L.)

MARIA (*stopping her*). Don't. Unless I'm very much mistaken, he's persuading Richard at this moment to take his clothes off for him.

HELEN. I wish I hadn't been so horrid to him.

MARIA. He's forgiven you, I'm sure. Nice little man, I misjudged him very much! (*Crosses to the settee.*)

HELEN (*going* L., *looking out*). Why doesn't Richard come back and tell me?

MARIA (*sitting on the settee*). I gather you still like him——

HELEN. Yes, I do. There's something about George you can't help liking, try as you will not to. Oh, why doesn't Richard come back?

MARIA. Patience, Helen dear.

HELEN. But I may be able to do something for him.

(RICHARD *re-enters and crosses* HELEN *to* R.C.)

Quickly—how is he?

RICHARD. Splendid!

MARIA (*angrily*). Splendid. How can a man be suddenly splendid who collapsed in this room a minute ago as he did?

RICHARD. Too healthy, I expect.

HELEN (L.C.). What do you mean?

RICHARD. His pulse is normal, no temperature—he's——

HELEN. But shouldn't one of us go and fetch a doctor at once?

RICHARD. That's a good idea. (*Crosses to* L.) I'll go and tell George to at once.

MARIA. Oh, you unsympathetic, horrid man!

RICHARD. Not at all. I made a marvellous suggestion to him—I pointed out to him in the event of this being a long illness how much nicer your room would be than the one he was in.

MARIA. Did he agree?

RICHARD. He didn't say—but he is in your bed.

MARIA. I'm glad.

RICHARD. Oh, I nearly forgot—in the midst of some curious noises he was making, which I thought was singing and which he explained to me were groans—he asked me to send you to him at once.

MARIA (*rising*). Why didn't you tell me that before?

RICHARD. I don't know—I was so upset to see old George looking so well I quite forgot it!

MARIA (*crosses to* L.). I would have never believed that there could be anyone in this world so cruel and as unsympathetic as you are! (*She quickly goes out* L.)

RICHARD (L.C.). Now's our chance.

HELEN (C.). Will you explain to me what all this means?

RICHARD. George doesn't want to leave you to-night.

HELEN. He's only pretending to be ill ?

RICHARD. And indifferently. (*Goes up* L.) Twice he had to put his head under the pillow to prevent me seeing him laughing. (*He walks to window, pulls curtains. It is snowing hard.*) In another hour nothing will be able to get away from here. (*He crosses at the back to the porch and takes a motor-coat and puts it on.*)

HELEN. Maria told me the other day that she and her husband were once snowed up here for three weeks.

RICHARD. Let us pray this time it will be a month.

HELEN (*standing by the chair* R. *of the table*). Is it fair to take the car and leave them without a chance in the world of getting away from here ?

RICHARD. Fair ? It's the kindest thing that has ever been done for them. Such hell as a month alone here together will make them the nicest people in the world. (*Gets hat and gloves—and takes another coat down for* HELEN.)

HELEN (*sitting*). It's a cruel thing to do.

RICHARD (*advancing to* HELEN *with the coat*). You mean you don't want to leave George ?

HELEN. I don't, very much.

RICHARD. Do you love him ?

HELEN. I think I do.

RICHARD. Then for Heaven's sake, do this for them ; and then, I believe I will be able to show you the two people we thought we liked. (*He puts the coat over her shoulders.*)

HELEN (*rising as she gets into the coat*). But it may kill them both !

RICHARD. It will cure them both !

HELEN. I knew when it really came to it I should be weak !

RICHARD. I implore you to believe that I am right.

HELEN. In my heart I know you are.

RICHARD (*going behind* HELEN *to the back of the table*). Of course I am. (*He places a letter on the table.*) Thank Heaven I won't be here when she reads that ! Ready ? (*He crosses to the porch.*)

HELEN. Yes, I hate doing it, but I know you're right. (*She follows him.*)

RICHARD. I know I am. (*He opens the porch door.*)

HELEN (*standing in the door*). Poor darling George !

RICHARD. Poor sweet Maria !

(*They exeunt, closing the door.*)

(MARIA *enters from* L., *expecting to find someone in the room.*)

MARIA (*calling*). Richard ! (*There being no answer she goes to the kitchen door and calls again. Then she goes out for a moment and returns.*)

(*Motor horn off.*)

(*She is moving to the window when she sees the letter on the table. She looks at the envelope, opens it, reads, and screams.*)

(*The* DUKE *enters* L.)

DUKE. Has no one got the decency to come and see a dying man ?

. (*Coming* C., MARIA *waves him away, unable to speak.*)

What's the matter ?

MARIA (C.). Read—read—read that ! (*Waves the letter towards him.*)

DUKE (*taking the letter and turning to* L.C. *Reading*). " Maria and George,—The snow is a foot deep—it will be deeper to-morrow.—At heart you are both very nice people, but what you need is six months before the mast as common sailors—to suffer the degradations of the poor, and know the humiliations of their hardships.—So that you may suffer all these things, and more, Helen and I leave you alone—we pray for at least a month."

(*He throws the letter down. Runs to the outer door ; opens it. It is snowing harder. He stands in the door, looking at something intently.*)

MARIA (*up* R.C.). Stop them ! Stop them quickly ! Oh, why don't you stop them !

DUKE (*shaking his head*). Because I can't run forty miles an hour.

MARIA. Have they gone ?

DUKE (*closing the door*). Even the lights of their car have disappeared. (*Moves down* L.)

(MARIA *screams and sits* R. *of table.*)

Don't make that row. I'll never speak to either of them again. (*He goes up* L. *to the window.*)

MARIA. Nor shall I. If I have to stay alone in this house with you—I shall go mad !

DUKE (*at the window*). Look at it ! Have you ever been snowed up here before ?

MARIA. Once, for three weeks !

DUKE (*at the back of the table*). Oh, heavens! will no one have mercy on us and come and deliver us from each other ?

MARIA. Nothing—nothing—will be able to get up that hill !

DUKE. And you and I alone here—until—(*points to window*) that stops ?

MARIA. Yes.

(The DUKE *moves over to the armchair* R. *of the fire and throws himself into it.)*

(There is a pause.)

(They both gaze into space.)

(MARIA *rises and crosses to door* L.)   I—I—shall go to bed until it does.

DUKE.   Only the snow will want to come in! You need not lock your door.

CURTAIN.

FURNITURE AND PROPERTY PLOT

ACT I

Mauve carpet. Long runner. Two black skin rugs. White bearskin rug.

Down stage R.—Small occasional table on which is set a tall vase with roses, a black cigar-box and cigars, ash-tray, match-stand and matches, and a book.

Above the door R.—A standard electric lamp.

In the R. *corner up stage.*—A baby grand piano, on which is set an ornamental cover, a small vase with roses, stand and bowl with roses, a silver cigarette-box and cigarettes, and a book.

In front of the piano.—A piano stool.

At the back of the piano.—A black pedestal with a small palm and roses.

On the rostrum at window.—A small chair, set R., and a china cabinet set C. between the windows.

Up stage L.C.—A small kidney-shaped table on which is set a P.O. telephone and silk cover, a stand and bowl with roses, and a copy of the " Tatler."

In front of the small table up L.C.—A small chair.

To the L. *of the small table.*—A standard electric lamp.

On the L. *wall below the standard lamp.*—A large china cabinet with glass front, on which is set a small stand and bowl with roses, and a tall vase with roses.

Against the wall below the cabinet.—A small chair.

At fireplace down L.—Club fender. Dogs and irons.

On the mantel.—Black bowl, two small black vases and stands, two silver frames, a small clock, a match-stand and matches.

Below the fireplace.—An armchair with a large cushion.

At the R. *down-stage corner of the hearthrug.*—A pouffe ottoman.

L. *of* C. *up stage.*—An oblong table on which is set a plated coffee service on tray, four cups and saucers, plated spoons, a cut-glass liqueur set, match-stand and matches, ash-tray, two glasses, whisky and brandy decanters, soda syphon and syphon-holder, and a small glass water-jug.

L. *of the oblong table.*—An armchair.

At the back of the table.—A small chair.

R.C. *down stage.*—A settee with arms and two cushions.

On the walls.—Five oval-framed drawings in colour.

Net curtains to the sashes and long curtains and pelmets to the windows.

Ivy on the balustrade outside windows.

All furniture painted satinwood.

ACT II

Blue carpet, two rugs, one black skin rug.

Down stage R.—An oak armchair.

Above the oak armchair.—Oak writing-desk, on which is set a metal inkstand and pens, stationery, blotting-pad, a tall vase and flowers, two brass candlesticks and candles.

In front of the desk.—A small oak chair.

On the wall above the lower door R.—A copper warming-pan.

In the porch up stage R.—Hat pegs on the R., a small oak chair on the L. and a small table behind the door.

On the R. *of the fireplace.*—A small table on which are some ornaments, a book, and a small jewel-case.

On the wall above the small table.—A small brass warming-pan.

At the fireplace C.—Fire-irons and dogs, a small hearth brush and a coal scoop, a small oak tray at its L. side.

On the mantelpiece.—Two tall candlesticks, four-branched candlestick and candles, small cigarette-box and cigarettes.

L. *of the fireplace.*—A standard electric lamp.

At windows L.C. *and* L. *up stage.*—Chintz-covered window-seats and cushions.

Between the windows.—An oak grandfather clock.

Against the wall below the windows.—An oak cabinet on which is set two brass candlesticks and candles, a vase and flowers, and on the shelf a key.

In the alcove entrance L.—A small oak chair and a large brass plaque on the wall.

Below the alcove entrance L.—Oak cabinet gramophone and double record.

In front of the gramophone.—A low four-legged stool.

Up stage L.C.—A large oak table on which is set a large knife and fork, dessert spoon and fork, a small knife, mat, napkin, a small plate of oat cake, salt and pepper casters, ash-tray, cigarette-box and cigarettes, a match-stand and matches, and an illustrated paper.

Behind the large table.—An oak armchair.

On the L. *of the fireplace.*—A large easy chair covered in chintz and a large cushion.

On the R. *of the fireplace.*—A large easy chair chintz covered, with large cushion.

R.C. *set up and down stage.*—A roomy settee with arms and large cushions.

On the walls.—Six oil paintings in dull gold frames.

On the shelf above ceiling beam.—Four pewter plates, two candlesticks and a trophy.

On the beam.—Pelmet and curtains.

Over alcove entrance L.—Pelmet and curtains.

On the wall above alcove L.—A stag's head and a pewter plate.

Pelmets and practical curtains to both windows.

Twelve-branch brass candelabra hanging C. in front of ceiling beam.

Set off stage R.—Dinner plate with food. Plate and bread. Butter-dish and butter. Plate of rice pudding. Shopping bag and four parcels. Telegram. Plated tea service on tray. Plate with cake. Muffin dish. Four cups and saucers. Four teaspoons. Cigar-case and cigars for DUKE. Crash to represent falling coal-scuttle. Wind machine. One snow-bag.

Set off stage L.—Two snow-bags.

ACT III

All curtains closed. Small chair from desk set R. end of the table up L.C.

Off stage R.—Letter for RICHARD.

White handkerchief for the DUKE.

Off stage L.—Leather suit-case.

Set in the porch.—Man's motor-coat, cap and gloves.

Woman's motor-coat, veil, and gauntlet gloves.

LIGHTING PLOT

Floats and Batten.—One circuit light pink, two circuits white.

ACT I

Float and batten full up.
Green floods on backcloth, P. and O.P.
One standard lamp up stage P. alight.
One standard lamp at down-stage door O.P. alight.
Two brackets on fireplace alight.
One bracket centre of windows alight.
Centre fitting and fire alight.

No Change.

ACT II

Float and batten full up.
Four floods open white P.S. window backing up stage.
One flood blue and frost on check up stage.
Two floods open white, door backing O.P. up stage.
One bracket P.S. not alight.
One bracket O.P. not alight.
Log fire and floor standard lamp not alight.
Cue 1 : (Gramophone).—Check to ½ all outside lighting.
Cue 2 : " Tell me the colour of my eyes "—Bring slowly up to ¾.
Cue 3 : " You are irritating me "—Bring up blue and frost lamp P.S. to ¾ and
    check outside lighting to down.
Check white circuits, float and batten to ½.

ACT III

Float and batten full up.
Brackets, floor standard and fire alight.
Two blue and two green floods at window backing P.S.
One blue and one green flood at door backing O.P.
Set motor effect O.P.
Set motor headlight effect at window P.S.
At Cue : When Maria *enters kitchen*—Motor effect. Followed by motor
    headlight effect on window P.S.

No Change.